D0451230

WILDERNESS

THE GATEWAY TO THE SOUL

SCOTT STILLMAN

WILDERNESS

THE GATEWAY TO THE SOUL

WILD
SOUL
PRESS

Wild Soul Press
Boulder, Colorado

Copyright © 2018 by Scott Stillman

The moral right of Scott Stillman to be identified as the author of this work has been asserted by him in accordance with the Copyright, Designs, and Patents Act of 1988. All rights reserved. Published in the United States by Wild Soul Press. No part of this book may be reproduced in any form or by any electronic or mechanical means, without permission in writing from the publisher, except by a reviewer who may quote brief passages for a review.

Design and layout: Andrea Costantine
Editors: Emma Murray, Alexandra O'Connell

Front Cover: Sierra Nevada Range (photo by Scott Stillman)
Back Cover: Dirty Devil WSA (photo by Scott Stillman)

Library of Congress Cataloging-in-Publication Data
Stillman, Scott
Wilderness, The Gateway To The Soul / Scott Stillman
LCCN 2018905920

ISBN: 978-1-7323522-0-9

WILD
SOUL
PRESS

Contents

Author's Disclaimer

This book does not contain any suspenseful scenes. There are no wacky characters. There is not a surprise ending. In fact, there really are no characters, and there really is no plot.

Still reading?

I wrote this book because it needed to be written. Simple as that. Our wilderness is shrinking at a terrifying rate. Someone needs to speak up for it. We all need to speak up for it. Or it will be gone.

I've set forth but one purpose. To tell the Truth. All that is not the Truth has been omitted. Edited out completely. What's left is what you see.

Mostly, this book attempts to answer a simple question. The most important question of all: Why?

Why save wilderness? Why do we need it? What purpose does wilderness serve in our technologically advanced world? Why bother at all?

Still here?

Good. Maybe this book has a chance. Go on now. Read the damn book. I hope it provides you with some spiritual entertainment, maybe even a few laughs. Mostly, I hope it gets you out *there*. Into wilderness.

WILDERNESS

THE GATEWAY TO THE SOUL

CHAPTER ONE

Indian Creek Wilderness, Utah

Why am I out here in this desert, all alone?
Why did I choose to put myself here?
My mind searches for an answer. Finds none.
It's cloudy, and the wind has picked up.

Wrapped in my sleeping bag,
I stare out to a sea of sandstone
Ripples, folds, peaks, and mounds.
They stretch out for miles,
Off to distant mountain ranges far beyond.

I'm here.

The stillness,
The silence,
It's absolute,
Deafening in its purity.

This land heals,
Cleanses the mind,
But first you must get away.
Away from the machines.
The Monsters.

It's possible,
But you must be willing to walk,
And it's worth it.

Gazing out to the red cliffs,
The black canyons, the cold sky,
I start to realize,
I've been here all along,
My entire life,
Just witnessing.

I have been here before.
In a canyon,
On a mountain,
And a sandy beach,
A thousand miles away.

I've been here many times.
Over and over I keep coming back,
Making my pilgrimage back to this place,
Where my mind stops making so much noise.

Where the details of my life melt away,
And all that's left is this moment,
Right here, right now.

My God. How long has it been this time?
How long since I've stopped this maddening
Chatter in my head?
Weeks? Months?

I stare out over the lost horizon,
Down into a maze of twisted rock, sand, and sky.

Floods of emotion.
Goosebumps.
Deep love, gratitude.

I have found God, Eden,
If just for now.

This is why I've come.

The desert, the mountains,
The sea and the sky,

They are my teacher.
Mother Nature herself.

Yes. I have been here before.
Not this exact point on the map,
But to this place where my thoughts stop,
And only beauty remains.

A vacation from the person I believe myself to be,
And a celebration of the one I am.

The one who doesn't come and doesn't go,
The one who is me and who is you,
And the rocks and the trees,
The animals and the plants,
The moon and the stars,
The sand in my notebook.

Time stops.

Have I ever left this place?
Have I been here all along?
I ask the rocks.
They seem indifferent. Yes? No?
What difference does it make, they seem to say.

A raven cries out.
I think I understand.

These incessant ramblings between visits,
Are they real?
Job, house, bills, computers, internet,
Thoughts, things, cravings, worries,
Thoughts, things, thoughts, thoughts...

They seem so far away now,
Like some other lifetime.

Clouds, darker now on the horizon.
A blanket of peace settles in.
I need nothing. I so need nothing.

The seed of enlightenment has been sown.
It must be watered to grow.

Morning.

Snow blankets the red rocks around my camp. Stillness. Cold. Thermometer reads 15 degrees Fahrenheit. I've camped under an overhang, good protection from last night's storm, but now I need the sun. I pack up early, crawling towards the warmth. The fiery ball emerges, painting my world with color—crimson, orange, lavender—against a backdrop of deep shadow and crystalline snow. I climb out onto a ledge, into the sun, warming my bones in the dazzling light. It's finally time to make coffee, watch the day unfold.

The snow around me sizzles like hotcakes on a sandstone griddle. Junipers sparkle like diamonds in the morning light. I'm wildly alert. Aware. A thought snakes its way into my consciousness, snapping me momentarily from the bliss. "Should've brought the camera." Then I remember, I forgot it on purpose. Just another distraction, another gadget for my mind to latch on to. I want to give all my attention to the desert. Submit to her completely. I don't want to photograph her, I want to become her.

CHAPTER TWO

Sycamore Canyon Wilderness, Arizona

THERE IS ONE PROBLEM with desert hiking in the late fall. Water. I'm already struggling to conserve.

It's day one of my five-day solo journey through the Arizona desert. I plan to hike from Cottonwood to Sedona, by way of Sycamore Canyon, a remote wilderness canyon. In Sedona, my wife and I will rendezvous at a local coffee shop where she will pick me up, about fifty miles from here. I brought four liters of water. I'm already down to one.

I'd planned to find more water in the canyon, preferably by sundown. Failed. Now there's no water for cooking, no tea, no morning coffee. Not to worry, these are minor inconveniences. Luxuries I can live without. It's the uneasiness in my stomach that's more of a problem. I can't stop thinking about water.

Morning.

In the gray morning light, before the rising of the sun, I pack up my gear and move on, avoiding the heat, skipping breakfast. I chew my options as I walk, considering my situation. I could simply return the way I came, certainly a possibility. It's nine miles back to Cottonwood, there was water there in Parsons Spring. But that would be backtracking, a last resort, putting an end to my trip. Perhaps I'll go on just a little further, there should be water ahead. Must be water ahead.

Onward.

The low sun creeps over the horizon, turning my canyon to blood. A passing hiker snaps me from a waking dream. He appears frazzled, his face red and sunburned, carrying a pack way too large for his build. I ask if he's seen any water. "No," he replies curtly, avoiding eye contact, focused on something else. Something far away.

Onward.

My trail becomes faint, then disappears altogether. Reappears. Disappears. Game trails lead in every direction, spidery routes that fizzle out into a web of nothingness, an animal logic I cannot begin to understand.

Retrieving my compass from the top of my pack, I point it north, in the direction of Sycamore Creek. On my map the creek is five miles from here, as the crow flies. Of course if I were a crow I could survey the land from above, scanning the horizon for water, shimmering pockets of life hidden deep within the rock. But as a human I'm destined to continue my search on foot, relying instead on my maps, smell, intuition—what little my species has left.

Late in the afternoon I find Sycamore Creek. Dry. Shit. I walk out into the center. It's scorched and black, every last drop of moisture sucked out long ago by a relentless Arizona summer. I stop and listen, for water, for anything. There is nothing. Nothing but my own last hot swig of water, sloshing around at the bottom of my bottle, in quiet desperation.

I have choices. Nothing is fucked. Not yet. I consult my map. I can still return the way I came, now fifteen miles back, in the wrong direction. The thought of it sounds dreadful, cruel, humiliating. There must be another way. My map shows an off-trail route, up and over a pass, down to a forest road. From there I might be able to hitch a ride back to Cottonwood, if there's anyone up there, *out there*, in this heat. I consider my predicament. Both choices are bad. Both require miles of backtracking through hot, dry, waterless terrain. Dry lips, dry tongue, dry... I try not to think about it.

There's this dry creek bed beneath my feet; perhaps my answer lies here, in Sycamore Creek. I trace it on the map, to see where it goes. If I follow it south it should lead back to Parsons Spring, forming an obscure loop, back to where I started, where there was water.

Without further thought, further deliberation, I hoist my pack over my shoulders and start walking, south, in the direction of Parsons Spring. A decision made more from instinct rather than logic, a method that has always served me in times like these.

Onward.

Hopping, leaping, bouncing from rock to rock, boulder to boulder, I dance my way through stones the size of basketballs and washing machines. Immediately I know I've made the right decision. I feel good, optimistic, energetic even after only a mile. Then I spot something glimmering in the rocks up ahead.

I find it crucial to maintain composure in moments like these. I don't know why but it is. I'm careful not to get too worked up. Not yet. I need to be sure.

Then I see birds. Diving down into a small hole in the granite, stopping for...

I come closer. The hole is two feet wide, four feet long, and deep. Remains from past rains. Water. More than I could drink in a week. Dead and dying bees, wasps, and flies float on the surface, drowning. Drowning in the desert.

I filter the water and drink it. It tastes cool, sweet, divine. I pump seven liters, filling every receptacle in my pack. Another liter gurgles in my full belly. For a while I just sit in silence and wonder. The canyon intensifies with a beauty I hadn't quite noticed before. Shadows deepen, colors saturate, the air sparkles, energy buzzes, finches flutter. I fall deeply into a state of pure joy, pure ecstasy.

Searching for water in the desert I find immensely satisfying. You don't often find it, but *man* when you do.

I celebrate with goat cheese, Wheat Thins, and espresso chocolate. Then I make some instant lemonade and soak in the sun, reading and relaxing. I set up my camp early, directly in the wash. With no rain in the forecast, a flash flood here is unlikely. Then I retrieve a book from my pack, an old beat-up paperback by Craig Childs. The words on the cover read, "There are two easy ways to die in the desert: thirst and drowning."

The next morning I make yet a new plan. I will revert back to my original route. With this much water I can now complete my trip. So it's onward to Sedona.

A newfound energy takes me over. I have two days of pristine desert walking ahead. I'm completely alone, of this I am sure. Besides the wearisome hiker on day one, I've seen no one. Just a few cat tracks and a single horned toad. He was not in the mood to chat, but did let me stroke his spiny forehead.

Walking. Rhythmic walking. When I'm backpacking I'm backpacking. There is nothing else. No phone to answer, no email to check, no bills to pay, no errands to run. Nothing but backpacking. Sure there's preparation, gear to sort, meals to plan, routes to ponder. But once I start walking, a peace takes over, a simple joy like none other I've ever known. There are no distractions. Nothing but Now.

I'm greeted with more game trails, more route finding, more bushwhacking, but the scenery is grandeur. Cream-colored cliffs, liver-colored canyons, sapphire-blue skies. Late in the afternoon I find the trail that leads up and out of this canyon. According to my map it's a 2,000-foot climb, straight up a ravine. I take it. Par for the course the route is difficult. Nothing more than an overgrown deer trail. Clinging to brush and weeds, I make my way up. The hillside crumbles as I hike at a snail's pace. Thorns claw my legs, blood trickles into my socks.

Halfway up the ravine I find a water pocket deep down in some large boulders, twice the size of the first. I carefully lower myself and receptacles down into the cold chamber, fill everything to capacity, and emerge. Heaving the massive load onto my back, my pack sways back and forth, digging at my shoulders, sloshing with gallons of water. Awkward for sure. But my mind is at peace. I find it a worthy trade. I'm no longer thinking about water.

I reach the top almost without noticing. Wearily, I look up as a new world emerges. The sight startles me as

I take a step back to refocus. I'd been staring at my feet for hours, now I can see for a hundred miles.

Layers and layers reveal themselves. Mountains, desert, sky. Blissful open sky. Sedona's Secret Mountain Wilderness lies beyond, mysterious and enchanting. There I will make camp for the night.

Hours later I make it to the edge of the wilderness. I find a nice place to camp with several more water pockets nearby. One contains a liter or two, the other is much larger containing five or six. Plenty enough for unlimited refills of coffee and tea. I relax for the remainder of the afternoon, resting my tired feet, washing the scrapes on my arms and legs, and savoring my surroundings. Tomorrow will be my last day, it's a fourteen mile walk back to Sedona.

Sketchy footing, tricky navigation, thorns and brush, twenty extra pounds of water on my back, this trip has been a test of character to say the least. But my energy levels have been high. I'm eating simple foods, nuts and dried fruit, rice and veggies. Walking for hours I breathe deeply, rhythmically. Blood pulsates through my veins, surging with vitality. I wake up early full of energy. I feel alive.

Rainstorm.

The clouds cave in. Violent thunder crashes around

me like freight trains charging from every direction. Then comes the hail, bouncing like marbles crashing against the rock. After days of crackling heat the desert is purified, cleansed, reborn. Every pocket and groove in the sandstone fills to capacity, then overflows. Celebration saturates the air as life fills the desert. I sit in my tent wide-eyed, awaiting the next explosion. I've camped next to a wash, an artistic masterpiece of sand and stone, sensual shapes and curves, fine arcs and tunnels carved into the rock, sculpted by thousands of years of wind and rain—just like this. I wonder if it will flood.

When the storm lets up I step from my tent. Water races down the various channels and grooves in the rock. Gallons of it surround me, where just a while ago, there was nothing but dry stone. As I stare at the bounty a rainbow paints itself across the sky. Mother Nature provides. She always provides. Thank you.

Morning.

Up at first light. Fog blankets my camp. It rained all night, filling several more pockets. Water is everywhere. Sipping coffee, I watch birds darting from pocket to pocket. Their movements are fast, imperceptible to the naked eye. Chipmunks hop from ledge to ledge, perfectly balanced; there is no hesitation, each move is precise, never a clumsy step. I think of myself just yesterday blundering down the side of the mountain, kicking rocks, sliding around, making all sorts of racket. I spy an ant crossing a path of branches and rocks many times his size. Gracefully he moves through the chaos without a sound. How do these creatures move with such grace, while I blunder and stumble through my day? Perhaps it's that these creatures have but just one thing to master. We on the other hand are jacks-of-all-trades, trying to do a thousand things, yet rarely attempting to master a single skill. I know that I must simplify. Learn what it means to master being human, perfection in every step, no hesitation, no thought, no ego.

An orange glow creeps through the fog and spreads over my camp like a warm fuzzy blanket. Rocks radiate in mystical light, dampness clings to the air, and a deep silence falls upon the land. My mind slows. Stops.

> The first things to drop away are the names...
> I no longer see a rock, a lizard, a tree,
> I only see.

The orange glow intensifies. To my back, billows of dark clouds obscure an expanse of soft hills, red cliffs, hazy mountain ranges. There is so much to see, just sitting. There is no need to go anywhere.

I find that when I open up and surrender to the present moment, accepting it for all its beauty and amazement, the universe guides me to all the right places. Decisions are just decisions. Either answer is correct. Just choose.

The universe will take care of us, provided we are grateful, aware. It's when we fight the present moment that the universe turns against us. Nothing goes our way. Every decision is wrong. We get caught up in our minds, our egos. "If only I had done this, or done that." Life becomes a struggle.

Today is a beautiful day. I think I'll hike to Sedona.

CHAPTER THREE

Uncompahgre Wilderness, Colorado

B LACK SHEETS OF RAIN. Thunder, hail, wind. At 12,000 feet it's cold, but I can't feel the sting through the walls of my tent, the warmth of my bag. Everything I need is right here, and within arm's reach. Sturdy tent, down sleeping bag, camp stove, puffy jacket, rain gear, fleece hat. Just the essentials. All I need to survive, nothing I don't. These items I carry cost less than my mortgage payment, and I own them—they are my security blanket.

When the economy goes to pot, I go walking. Recession, layoffs, unemployment? All good reasons to hit the trail. We worry about so much when freedom is right outside the door. And the gear is remarkable. Everything today is comfortable, lightweight, sturdy. Gone is the heavy, leaky canvas of the '80s. We can now walk where we wish, in total comfort. This is the golden age of outdoor gear.

When winter comes, simply follow the birds, heading south where it's warm. Start walking in October and you'll be basking in the southern sun by December.

Nonsense!

This is the golden age of convenience, ease, and luxury as well! Far better to take the train, the plane, the bus. Hitchhike! We live in the easiest, most comfortable time to be alive. Never before has the nomadic lifestyle made so much sense.

There will, of course, be expenses. Like food, for example. So it's best to learn a trade, something useful. Learn to repair something, or cook, farm, construct, play music, sing, dance, weave, heal, bake. Your services will be needed along the way, take them with you, but first you must lose the baggage. Lose the gadgets, and the bills that come with them, and go buy some decent backpacking gear. For less than a month in the city the world can be yours.

> I can lose my house,
> Lose my job,
> Lose my car,
> Lose my wallet.
> But I can always go backpacking.

Evening.

There exists a heaven. Not in some far-off realm high above the clouds, but here, right here on Earth. A place where the grandest of cathedrals are created, not by man, but by the very hands of God. An island in the sky where stone monuments shoot straight up out of the Earth, granite towers rise 6,000 feet into the clouds, and living hills of lush green velvet roll on for miles. Jade waterfalls cascade down their slopes, one after another, after another. A place of limitless abundance and impossible beauty.

A shark's fin blocks out the sun, six hundred feet tall. A granite castle dominates the view behind me, and rushing water engulfs the basin with sound. Then there are the trees. The trees! In all my life I've not seen trees like this. The pines stand like giants, a hundred feet tall and three feet in diameter, well-spaced with plenty of room to breathe. The aesthetic placement of these pines is a work of sheer artistic brilliance. Wildflowers dance, the soil breathes, and the entire forest sparkles with glistening water droplets. Cow Creek Canyon lies far below, dark and mysterious, so remote and inaccessible that trails only exist on the rim. Nothing leads down into the abyss.

It's Saturday night, and for all the Jeeps, SUVs, ATVs, OHVs, and SOBs on the road leading up to Engineer Pass, no one's up here, out here, in this wilderness. They're all down at the campgrounds, camped in RVs, watching satellite TV. I've camped there too, out of necessity, on my way somewhere else. When it gets dark, everyone goes inside. Then I am alone, sipping a Jack and Coke, surrounded on all sides by glowing, grumbling machines— metal boxes made from recycled beer cans. Inevitably a generator kicks on, killing the silence. I turn on some music but it's of no use, the noise is all-consuming. The night is lost. I fetch some ear plugs and fall asleep to the closed-off silence inside my head.

Darkness washes over the basin. Unrelenting stillness. Wrapped in my bag I listen to the night. An animal makes an eerie sound like a loud whisper. I heard this same sound earlier while walking. I thought people were approaching so I stopped and turned around. "Hello?" There was nothing. Nothing but the hollow sound of my own voice. Strange. Empty. Insignificant.

I drift off to the voices in the gurgling stream. Following them downriver. Into the unknown.

Storms.

Thunder barrels through the canyons, echoing off the walls of petrified skyscrapers. Rain pounds against tent fabric, saturating my dreams in an ocean of sound. The storm is alive, a living, raging organism. Rather than a witness, I feel myself part of it. I'm no longer sure what's real and what's fantasy, where the dreams end and reality begins, or if there is even a difference.

Awake again. Water droplets rhythmically hit my forehead. Tap. Tap. Tap. Condensation raining down on me from the roof of my tent, caused by the heat of the morning sun. Rays of light stream through the door, blinding me as I open my eyes. A low fog blankets the morning in a purple hue. I climb out to prepare coffee. The air is brisk, magical. An elk bugles, a hummingbird buzzes, and I'm overwhelmed with intense gratitude. It's a new morning, and a great day to be alive.

Beyond this island in the sky, over the ledge, one world disappears and another begins. I crawl out on my hands, knees, and stomach to get a closer look. When I peer over I freeze at a glimpse of inescapable beauty. Cow Creek Canyon plummets 4,000 feet, straight down to the canyon floor. This is Earth in its most raw state of natural beauty, perfection in every detail, terrain that can never be tamed, nor developed. Too wild. Too unreachable. Too sacred. Any improvement here would be devastation.

There is nowhere to hide. My alertness borders on intoxication, my senses excruciating. I think I've found the heart. The living, beating heart of this place. Not a single thought passes through my mind for what seems like an eternity. If the Holy Grail exists, I have found it. My very reason for existence, and reason I've come. Reality jerks me back into itself. How long can I tolerate such beauty? Such bliss? Before it swallows me whole, devouring me until I become a part of it myself. I'm not sure I'm ready for that. Not yet.

I drift back to camp, tiptoeing through manicured gardens of rosy pink, crimson, lavender. Flowers mastering the art of being flowers. Marmots cry out from the boulder fields, poking their heads up out of the rocks in curious mischief, calling and answering to one another from across the valley. They navigate an organic infrastructure of tunnels, chambers, and underground passageways that offer protection from their predators, the weather, and the harshness of a long winter. A harshness we will never know. Retrieving my notebook I add *Marmot* to the list of animals I wish to be in another life. The Raven is first, and for obvious reasons. Masters of gravity and flight, they can soar on the thermals for hours, diving down a thousand feet, just to ascend again. Climbing. Descending. Reaching the highest peaks with a single swoosh of their wings. They have mastered the art of being Ravens.

As a human I'm happy enough to climb the peaks in my mind. I see no need to summit. They look majestic enough from down here in the valleys. Besides, I have other agendas. Like how much ecstasy did I feel? How closely did I inspect the ferns, clovers, and tiny gardens of plant life under my feet? I'm not here to tame or conquer, I'm here to connect. To find the gateway. I know it's out here. If I'm not careful I could miss it.

There is wisdom in anarchy, precision in chaos. Everything here is in its perfect place yet precisely out of order. Straight lines and boxes—the world growing tired of them. Correct grammar, a complete sentence? I don't want a complete sentence. I want to feel! Words that pierce my soul. Give me that one magically placed word that stops me dead in my tracks, forcing me to stop reading, and tremble. Transcendence! That's all I ask. Is that too much? And please, I don't want to hear another song played note-for-note, lyric for lyric, in perfect key and tone. I want to hear the key of life! Give me that one magically placed note, at the most precisely perfect moment in time, that is so fresh, so unexpected, that I'm awakened. Enlightened! If only for a moment. The flash of an instant.

There is much to be learned here. So much to be learned, from the undisturbed, incomparable, Uncompahgre Wilderness.

CHAPTER FOUR

Powderhorn Wilderness, Colorado

I DRIVE SEVEN HOURS into the night. From Boulder straight through to San Cristobal Lake, down in southern Colorado. When I arrive it's dark and I camp right on shore, the stars the only illumination I require. The lake is silent, and for a long time I sit and watch the stillness. A fish splashes. A mouse scurries. A moth inspects my shoulder, drawn to the light, like us all. When the moon finally arrives, I ease my inflatable paddleboard out into the water and paddle out into the darkness. The narrow beam of my headlamp slices through the night. When I switch it off I'm alone in a sea of stars, reflecting off the water, out into infinity. I can no longer differentiate between water and sky. There is no end.

I stand out in the darkness.
Floating. Weightless.

In the morning I drive on. San Cristobal Lake was just a stopover. I'm on my way up higher, into the San Juans, and the start of my trek into the remote Powderhorn Wilderness. The trip is long overdue. Southwestern Colorado is far from Boulder, but that's not a good excuse for my absence. I need to take longer trips. There's a lot out there to explore, and time is running out.

Camp.

Sipping from a small bottle of Pyrat rum, I stare out to the glow of the San Juans. Alpine meadows turn purple, then bronze in the setting sun. The air is cool but the rum warms my soul, easing me into the night.

Clouds turn from bronze, to pink, to lavender, blanketing my camp in an ethereal glow. An elk moves through fading light into the distant tundra.

I breathe slowly, fully, naturally. The other world is starting to melt away, but no euphoric moments yet, this is just day one. The distractions are gone, that's a good start. I carry only the necessities, plus this small bottle of rum. Because here I'll appreciate it. Taking another sip, I savor the sweet, smoky flavor.

I inhale deeply,
Taking in the silence,
Until I can take no more.

Then I let it all out.
Everything.
Until there's nothing left.

I wait.
For what I don't know.
But I wait.

The light fades,
Ever so slightly,
Changing everything.

Clouds build,
A bird chirps,
Another answers.

Morning.

Long, rainy night. I make a pot of strong coffee, grateful for the clear skies and warm air. When the coffee is ready I pour myself a cup and read a few pages of the paperback I've brought with me. Alan Watts talks of humans and potatoes. Who is more civilized? Alan makes a fine argument for the potato...

"Well," we might say, "how can it be? It has no civilization. It has no house. It has no automobiles. It has no pianos, no art galleries, no religion."

But the potato might say, "I don't need them. It's you poor uncivilized human beings who have all this crap around you to tell you who you are and what it's all about. You are messy and inefficient, and you are cluttering up the planet with all your culture. But I, the potato, have it all built into me."

"Well," we might say, "that's impossible, because you're stuck in one place all the time. Now how can you know anything about the world?"

But the potato doesn't need to go running around because its sensitivity extends all over the place. And so it might say, "I want to introduce you to a few things. There is my neighbor over here, the thistle. Have you ever seen how my thistle neighbor gets around? It has tiny seeds with down sticking out all over them, and when the wind comes these seeds float off into the air. And my neighbor the maple tree has little helicopters it sends off, and they spin in the air and fly away. And then I have a friend the apple tree, and it has fruit that is so delicious that the birds like it. They eat the apple and swallow the seeds, then they fly away and when they drop the seed it is sown."

These are incredible devices. Others have

burrs that stick in the hides of deer, and they carry these seeds around. "This is one of the ways we get around and we spread our people so that we aren't all crowded together and don't strangle ourselves."

The potato would go on to explain, "But this is only the beginning of the extraordinary things that we do. We have vibrations going on inside our fibers that are quite as good as anything invented by your Bach and Mozart. We enjoy this, and although you may think we are not doing anything because we just sit here all the time, we are vibrating, and we are in ecstasy. We are humming to the great hum that is going on everywhere." (Watts 2000, p. 36-38)*

I'm convinced. Closing the book, I look around and see the world with a powerful new sense of compassion. A true empathy. We *understand* each other. A heartwarming love develops, not just from inside of me, but all-encompassing of everything around me. I'm a visitor but welcome. We share the same space: the trees, the sun, the flowers, the water, the sky, the breeze. We all buzz with energy.

Or perhaps it's just the coffee.

*. From the book *Still the Mind*. Copyright © 2000 by Mark Watts. Reprinted with permission from New World Library, Novato CA. www.newworldlibrary.com.

Afternoon.

Storms approaching from the north. Camp is set and I'm ready. Let the show begin. My body is tired from a day spent navigating mountain passes, scree fields, and tundra. I could use some down time, but for now it's just threatening clouds, dark skies, rumbling thunder. I'm camped at treeline, 12,000 feet above the sea. Next to me is a black lake lined with lava rock. A lone tree holds my bear rope and food, silhouetted against a pale afternoon sky. Jagged outcroppings cut sharply through fields of vibrant green tundra. Swaying grasses and yellow flowers bow to the breeze. Views of the San Juan, Elk, and Sawatch mountain ranges extend off into the distance. I'm miles off-trail. Solitude is guaranteed.

To say this place is lightly traveled is an understatement. No one is here. What little trail exists is faint and overgrown. My kind of place. Across the valley a herd of elk grazes peacefully on a steep grassy slope. After a few minutes they notice me and take off running. Before disappearing beyond view, the entire herd stops, and in unison they swivel their heads back towards my camp. I show no sign of attack, taking another sip of my tea. They take off in a frenzy anyway, out into the valleys below, away from the threat they perceive myself to be.

The rain comes, heavy and ferocious. Large drops beat the roof of my tent and I feel like I'm inside of a drum. This continues for hours as I lie on my back in a chamber of sound. Feelings of loneliness, cravings for soft skin, soothing music, cold beer. Typical for day two. The cravings will pass. *Try to stay in the moment.*

My tent is leaking. Not a good sign.
I time the drops. One per minute.

Just before dusk the rain stops. I get a wild hair and run out into the alpine tundra, dancing into the fading light. I've been cooped up for hours, now I'm bursting with energy! The air is silent but waves of beautiful improvisational music stream from my memory banks, thousands of hours of music, catalogued, indexed, stored away neatly for remote listening. Oh the beauty and wonder of the human mind! Purple rain sways like curtains in the distance. I've transcended! Completely alone, yet held tightly in the arms of Wilderness. Mother Nature herself. God.

Waves of ecstasy, moments of clarity.
Gratitude. Freedom.
This place exists!
She's always here!
Patiently awaiting our return.

Even if we never come,
She exists just the same.

Sometimes that is enough,
Just knowing she is here.

Morning.

So much is happening in my meadow. Bugs of every conceivable color, shape, and size—they all come buzzing by, stopping to investigate my blue pack, my red water bag, my yellow hat. Thankfully none of them seem to bite or sting. Clouds drift passed in all their various formations. The sun beams down and a moderate breeze has the plants and flowers in a continuous dance.

I decide to inspect the black lake. Upon close examination I see that it provides housing for an array of species: butterflies, spiders, lizards, rodents. Eagles and hawks soar overhead, elk and deer wander through. All of this in my tiny meadow!

I sit on a rock watching the magic unfold. If I were to die in this moment what would really change? I would be as I was before I was born, forty short years ago. The flowers will still dance, the butterflies will still flutter, the hawks will still soar. But who to contemplate them? Perhaps a small child in a similar meadow on a similar day.

A sinking feeling.
Deep inside my gut.

This body wants to survive, continue on, as all life wants to persevere. It's the nature of all things. Yet I can't help but wonder if in our final moment there is a surrender. If just before the rabbit is eaten by the coyote, there is a flash of peace, a moment of understanding. A transformation will occur, yes, but life will go on, just the same.

When I sit and fully surrender to this moment, I know, without any doubt, that as long as there is life, I too will exist. That I will go on, just the same.

In all this open space it's so easy to think and to breathe. I'm far from the tangle of the thick forests below. I can see weather approaching from a hundred miles, fizzling out before it ever makes it here. There are no humans (besides myself), no machines, no roads, no developments. Just Wilderness. Heartbreakingly pristine Wilderness. The landscape is vast, like the desert, yet with temperatures much more suitable for July. Highs in the sixties, lows in the twenties. Intense sunshine in the morning, storms in the afternoon.

Wildlife at this elevation I find fascinating. These animals can walk, crawl, or fly where they wish, but they choose to be here, 12,000 feet above the sea. Many could not survive anywhere else. Pikas and marmots are among the most prevalent. You won't find a marmot below tree line. They waddle around in their fur coats announcing their presence to anyone passing through. What are they trying to tell us? "Hey there, give us your food," is a likely guess. An unattended food bag is more likely to be snatched up by a marmot than a bear at this elevation. Or perhaps they're simply saying to the other marmots, "Look, there's a human." The same way we would say, "Look, there's a marmot."

I should go for a hike.

What is stopping me? First I would need to make lunch, and that requires pumping water. This dilemma I've been contemplating off and on now for a few hours. Instead I continue to sit, surveying my surroundings. If I move I may miss something. A colorful bird. A moment of clarity. Thoughts of the *other world* may creep in. Much better to sit. Breathe deeply. Witness.

At home I'd be frantically looking for something to do. Catching up on emails, Facebook, the bank account, the weather. Time is precious, we shouldn't waste it. Really? Is time precious? What's more precious, time or the present moment? Up here clock time is gone. Distractions are gone. In their place—peace, pure essence. The essence of life. I'm content to let things be as they are. If it rains let it rain. If it's windy let it blow. Everything I need I have. There is nothing else to even decide, apart from should I eat, should I drink, should I pee? Besides basic survival nothing has to be done at all. The brain takes a well-deserved rest and meditation becomes my reality.

What if there were a secret back-door portal to enlightenment? A shortcut, so to speak. I believe that the answer lies here, in wilderness. The shortcut is the long walk. However, you must go it alone. Once you get past the jitteriness of day one, the cravings of day two, and the loneliness of day three, meditation comes easily and naturally. Months of tension can be released in just a few days.

Work?
Stress?
Bills?
The past?

What past?
Everything is perfect now,
And when is it ever not now?

I sit in wonder and amazement.

Here I am.
This is me.
This is who I am...

Evening.

Breathing. Humming. Humming and breathing. I sit on a bluff overlooking a creek, the sound of rushing water consumes the landscape, saturating the valley. A moose appears, jet black against a glowing hillside in the evening sun. He makes his way across the valley, barking quite like a dog, a strange and eerie sound I've never before heard. Moments later he's gone, vanishing into an aspen forest.

The sun becomes intense, low now on the horizon as it starts to set. It dips behind a mountain, covering me in shadow as it retreats to the other side.

When darkness comes I see shooting stars and the clouds of the Milky Way, all in clear view above my camp. I'm much lower in elevation now and the warm air is welcome. I fall asleep in the grass. The sounds of the creek carry me away on a blanket of liquid dreams.

CHAPTER FIVE

Dark Canyon Wilderness, Utah

I'M GOING DOWN-beneath the surface. An obscure path marks my way—rock cairns, ledges, arrows carved into the rock. It descends quickly, fifteen hundred feet in less than a mile. Soon it deteriorates to nothing more than a broken staircase of loose rocks and boulders the size of washing machines. The temperature on the rim was a pleasant seventy-two, halfway down it's a blistering ninety.

Heat exhaustion takes hold quickly in the desert sun. I take shelter under a boulder, squeezing myself into a body-sized cavity, the only shade I can find. In the fetal position I sleep. The desert crackles and sizzles around me, but the shade is welcome. In twenty minutes I awake, my skin cold and clammy. I crawl back into the fire. The blaze gives me a sudden rush, a deadly blast that's at once menacing, yet strangely invigorating. I continue through the jumble, down towards the canyon floor. There will be water and shade, if I can get there. If I just keep moving.

I feel as though I'm getting close to something. But what? Maybe it's an end, or a new beginning, a cross-roads perhaps, a time to choose. But choose what? Or maybe not to choose, just give up, latch onto a feather in the wind, and set sail on the breeze. Life. Is it a struggle or a breeze? Lately I seem to be choosing struggle, a complex web of thoughts and ideas crashing into each other all at once. I can feel myself drifting further and further into the black hole of incessant mind noise.

As I approach the canyon floor the noise in my head begins to subside, drowned out by the soothing sounds of cool running water. It's cascading down-canyon, winding its way through smoothly polished channels in the sand-stone, filling up swimming holes the size of bathtubs. In the shade of a cottonwood, I rest under its rustling leaves, trying to grasp onto my new surroundings. It's now that I realize the descent from hell has led me to the Garden of Eden.

For the next five days this oasis in the desert will be my home. The rocks, the lizards, the frogs, they will be my sole companions. Endless miles of twisting sandstone canyon will be all the entertainment I require. No maps will be necessary. The golden ribbon of water beneath my feet will be my only guide. Or I may just sit on this beach and not go anywhere. Decisions are gone. I left them back at the car. I have no use for them here.

"When you travel, you experience,
in a very practical way, the act of rebirth."
– Paulo Coelho

Morning.

I sleep in late. The sound of running water consumes me and I feel like I could sleep for days. I have found refuge. I have found peace. Deep within the cracks and fissures of the Earth.

Am I just a hopeless romantic with insatiable wanderlust? "Do what you love," people tell me. I love walking desert canyons. How to do *that* for a living? This I've been trying to figure out for half a lifetime.

"The good fight is the one we fight
because our heart asks it of us."
– Paulo Coelho

A few miles down-canyon I ditch my gear and make a basecamp. Losing the pack gives me a newfound freedom. Instead of hiking around the deep pools and waterfalls, I can now swim through them, climbing up the cascades, with cool water splashing me in my face. A pure delight in the heat of the afternoon.

Carved into a limestone bench, I find an emerald pool and spend all day there swimming, writing, making tea, and taking naps by the water. In the late afternoon I explore several more side canyons. The temperature is a comfortable ninety, morning till night. I spend my days in shorts, or nothing at all. At night, a cotton T-shirt provides all the warmth I need. My days are long and luxurious. They seem to go on forever.

Each night around five o'clock the light show begins. Beams of sunlight slice through the trees, bouncing off the canyon walls in a dancing display. For hours the show goes on. Strolling through the mystic, I happen upon a family of bighorn sheep. Drinking peacefully at the water's edge, in the sparkling light, they pause, glance my way for a moment, then casually go back to their business, apparently unthreatened by my presence.

Back at camp the dry desert breeze smooths my wrinkled, waterlogged skin. Walking and swimming through waterfalls, plunge pools, and hanging gardens, I've made my way through some of the most dramatic desert scenery I've ever seen. Life is everywhere—frogs, tadpoles, lizards, blue jays, finches, canyon wrens, ravens, bighorn sheep, squirrels, chipmunks, butterflies, dragonflies, and hummingbirds, to name a few. Tropical groves of tall grasses and reeds flourish in one canyon, sensual curves of solid sandstone dominate the next. An everchanging landscape. My days are long, wet, happy.

Dark Canyon. The name has haunted my dreams for years. A jungled mess of swirling contour lines on my Utah map. This place is all about the timing. It's always too early or too late. In the spring, mud and snow block the access roads. In the summer, heat scorches the canyon to a near lethal level. There's a short window. I'll take June. To truly embrace the water aspect of this canyon it must be hot, but not too hot. Ninety degrees feels just about right, once I'm on the floor, under the cottonwoods, in the water.

Then there's the evenings. The evenings! As the air cools, rocks and sand keep radiating heat for hours, creating the most lavish of climates. Hours of blissful evening relaxation welcome the desert wanderer in June.

"You're out there. Doing what you would die for.
Believing, till there's no turning back."
– Jay Farrar

Wilderness. My problems are over the moment I step out onto the trail, pack loaded, schedule free. For the next few days everything will be new. The past no longer matters, the future disappears, and the present moment comes at me frame-by-frame, in extreme high-definition.

It's the one place I feel completely at peace.

I've had no revelations. No epiphanies. No new directions revealed. Just the knowing that *this is right.* I was born to walk the Earth, experience the amazing beauty of this planet, and witness the splendor and magic of all things—to be overwhelmed by a ray of sunlight, touched by an encounter with a frog, and mystified by the texture of a rock wall. I was born to splash through the creeks, sing through the canyons, laugh with the squirrels, just as I did as a small child in the woods behind our family's home. I was born to be a kid, and not take life too seriously, or get sidetracked by a career, a project, or anything that ties me down to the life of bills, shiny new toys, status, and pavement.

> *"The best thing you've ever done for me, is to help me*
> *take my life less seriously. It's only life after all."*
> *– Indigo Girls*

Morning.

Steaming coffee in hand, I take an early morning walk down-canyon to a large swimming hole. The sun has not yet risen, and as I stroll, the smooth limestone cools my bare feet. When the sun emerges over the east canyon wall, I slip into the water. The morning sun warms my back. Afterward I lie beside the pool to dry off. A symphony of sound rings down from the trees as birds celebrate a new day rising.

I return for breakfast. Hash browns, sautéed bell peppers, summer sausage. Decadent. Heading upstream this time, I splash through the water, laughing at the glory of this day unfolding. Frogs jump, tadpoles scatter, lizards scurry. Further up-canyon, a series of channels carved into multicolored stone form three waterfalls, each flowing into a kidney-shaped swimming pool. On the edge of the upper pool I let my legs dangle over the falls.

What now? There's nothing. Nothing left to be done. If happiness is wanting what you have, I have found it. The canyon is even more beautiful than I'd imagined. Wild. Expansive. Enchanting. I could spend weeks down here.

This water has washed my busy mind clean. My thoughts, which only a few days ago were so numerous and complex, are now quite clear, focused, and precise. My soul is cleansed, my body is filled with gratitude, and all aspects of myself are peaceful and relaxed. I'm satisfied enough with the occasional passing breeze across my face, no other stimulation is necessary. I've stepped right into this moment, where everything is functioning perfectly all around me, and all I have to do is happily observe. Judgment is gone. Clock time is gone. In their place—buzzing life energy. My heartbeat is slow. My breath is full, healthy, effortless. I go deeper...

The breeze stops,
Stillness prevails,
But the sound of water remains,
It's a new kind of silence.

The silence, it's everywhere,
In the sound of thunder,
On a busy street,
And in the roar of a freight train.

The key is to listen,
To the silence behind the sounds,
The silence within.

Like dancers in sequins, the cottonwoods dazzle and sparkle against an illuminated backdrop of glowing red sandstone. Such a glory to witness! What's so comforting, so reassuring, so gratifying, is the fact that this happens every day, whether I'm here or not. The beauty remains. Perfection exists! Unfathomable. Unconditional. Long before we ever existed, long after we are gone. This place remains.

There are no roads, no motors, no scenic roped-off viewpoints, no paved walkways. No *improvements*. There's only one thing to improve here. Our respect. Our empathy. For the Earth. The very soil beneath our feet. This place we all come from, and will all return to, as does everything that nourishes our bodies to survive.

When I die I'll return to the soil, to be born again, perhaps next time as a flower, a tree, a frog, or if I'm lucky, a high soaring bird.

We come from the Earth. We return to the Earth. It happens over and over and over. You might say, we are the Earth. We've only to step away from our world of plastic and concrete to understand.

CHAPTER SIX

Wind River Range, Wyoming

A PICTURE MAY BE WORTH a thousand words, but words on a page can capture what an infinite number of photos cannot. Not merely a still image, but the living, breathing soul of a place. I intend to test this theory over the next several days in Wyoming's Wind River Range. Not with camera and lens, but with pen and notebook.

It's not just her beauty I wish to capture, but her message. Her mere reason for existence. I love her for her beauty, I'd be lying if I said I did not. She has a beauty beyond comprehension—intoxicating and powerful, leaving me weak in the knees, speechless, unable to express my infatuation. My devotion. She *is* beauty. Yet beyond her beauty lies the most profound spiritual presence I've ever known.

Everything here is in a constant state of flux. Weather can change in an instant. Thunderstorms, hail, snow, blue sky stillness. All is possible. All is welcome. I'll be out here for six days; I'm likely to experience it all.

A storm approaches from the east. Just in time. Camp is set and everything is ready. Bring on the storm. My last camping trip was too ambitious. We were a group of four with fixed plans and a tight schedule. Hiking morning to night we'd arrive at camp exhausted, with only enough energy left to fix dinner and crawl into our tents. This will be a lazy trip with no fixed agenda. The way I prefer it.

I'm situated on a lake peninsula, surrounded by a body of water called Dad's Lake. A grove of blue spruces shelter me from wind and the rain. This place is a sanctuary: chipmunks, squirrels, dragonflies, butterflies, gray jays (camp-robbers), and ducks (with babies in tow), all frolic in view of my private lagoon.

Dad's Lake is a happy place. There are inlets, coves, nooks, beaches, islands, and lagoons. The backdrop is jagged peaks, low-lying clouds, and bluebird sky. A few colorful tents dot the shoreline as anglers cast their lines for trout.

Thunder builds to a constant rumble. The wind picks up, bringing with it the storm. The rain comes in all at once, in buckets rather than drops. I lie in my tent, giddy like a child in a blanket fort, safe and protected, far away from the real world. I think of the many tents of my childhood. Sheets, blankets and rugs, draped over chairs and dressers, tables and lamps. Everything anchored by TV sets, boomboxes, vases and typewriters, whatever we could find. It's a wonder we made it out alive. But we were protected, in our secret world, our sanctuary. For hours we'd hide out in these makeshift fortresses, safe from chores, homework, the grownups. Not much has changed I suppose, just a bigger playground.

The rain stops as abruptly as it began. In ten minutes the sun is back out, turning my tent into a sauna. The heat is welcome but soon it will be overbearing, forcing me back out into the world.

When evening comes, more and more anglers appear around the lakeshore. I start to feel my soul beckoning for more solitude, more exploration. The mountains are calling. Quickly I break down camp, stuff my sleeping bag and tent into my pack, and move on. As I stroll the sun starts to set, casting its orange glow over the horizon. I follow a gurgling stream through a lush valley, until it opens up into an alpine basin. Here I wander far off-trail, out across the open tundra, and pitch my tent in the grass under the wide-open sky.

In fading light, I prepare stir-fry (brown rice, zucchini,

soy sauce, cashews). The meal is so satisfying that I find myself overwhelmed by emotions of gratitude and abundance. They surge through my body with a pulsing energy that races through every cell, every vein.

How lucky am I? This cathedral. This wonderland. These lush valleys and flower-filled meadows. I have them all to myself. Everything I could possibly need is right here by my side: a week's worth of delightful food, all neatly packed and organized; my efficient stove for preparing meals; my tent, featherweight, yet strong enough to withstand the rain, wind, and storms; and my goose down sleeping bag, keeping me cozy warm when temperatures dip below freezing. It all fits comfortably on my back.

Many consider this roughing it, but I'd beg to disagree. This is lavish decadence. I'm free from the demands of city life. I have endless opportunity to wander at will, or simply sit and watch the magnificence of creation unfold. It's all right here, happening before my very eyes.

Like the endless summers of childhood, my days are long, enchanting, and full of possibility. This is not roughing it. This is smoothing it.

Morning.

Clouds release and expand, bloom and uncurl, painting the sky with an ever-changing work of abstract brilliance. Meadowlarks sing, chipmunks bark, and I'm startled by a *whoosh!*—the wings of a hawk—just over my head. The sonic quality of this mountain air is crystalline, each delicate sound audible in extreme high-definition. I hear the footsteps of a grasshopper, the wings of a dragonfly, the trickle of a stream over a mile away. Pure potential unfolds right before my eyes. I'm locked into the now. My mind settles into a state of absolute awe, where the past no longer matters, and future doesn't even exist.

Some would call my experience meditation, but the word itself I find too distracting. If meditation is something you do, then this is quite the opposite. There is no trying here. No doing. Only sitting, observing, stillness, and splendor. I drift on the waves of a mountain breeze, in the vapor of a floating cloud, upon the wings of a soaring hawk. Energy buzzes through my every cell.

Meditation. One word, so difficult to define. Is it to do or not to do? Latch on to or let go? Are there rules? To properly meditate, must we sit still in a full lotus position, must we do yoga, or attend church? What about fishing? Can fishing be meditation? How about swimming, baking, tennis, golf?

Perhaps meditation is simply anything we do with our full attention, full awareness, full heart. Anywhere we find truth, or love. Something we do, not to be the fastest, or the best, or to win a prize, or to make a lot of money, but simply because we love it. Whatever *it* may be.

How many of us are trying to love what we do not love?

When we find true love, the trying disappears.

I think I've crossed a threshold. The land has now opened up to me completely, revealing her most intimate secrets, her most sacred beauty. Around every corner blossoms a new landscape, each more magnificent than the last. Pyramids, domes, castles, and monuments rise before me as I walk. Indigo butterflies dot the path ahead of me, iridescent in the midday sun; I must walk carefully to avoid them. Even the jays have changed. Down in the campgrounds their feathers were scruffy, their eyes sunken, their bodies nourished by bits of Cheetos, PowerBars, candy wrappers. Here their feathers are oily smooth, and their eyes sparkle with energy.

I wander along narrow streams and steep gullies, then beside wide rivers and open meadows. The water snakes its way through the waving grass, reflecting the blue sky and clouds overhead. Lining the streams are wild gardens of red, white, purple, and yellow wildflowers. This is high summer. The greatest time to be alive.

Animals scanter about with such exuberance and vitality. So full of spark! Chasing one another, playing, singing, celebrating, announcing their joy and existence to the world. A long snowy winter lies ahead, but today you would not know it. Our own food, shelter, and basic necessities we take for granted in our world of relative ease and luxury. Most of us will never know of real struggle, grumbling about the economy while sitting in the warmth of our homes, our cabinets stocked with food, complaining there's nothing to eat. Watching these animals today, you would never know of the real challenges they face. They soak up the present moment for all its glory. Frolicking in the joys of summer.

Evening.

Sun-dried tomato pesto, quinoa, toasted pine nuts, snow peas. I eat slowly, savoring the flavors of the Mediterranean, delighting in the fact that every time I eat, my pack gets lighter. At the start of a wilderness trip my load is heavy and awkward, but as my trip progresses the heaviness subsides, and an air of lightness takes over. My pack becomes welcome as an old friend, helping me along the trail, keeping me well-fed, warm, and happy.

I prepare tea. A soft light fills the basin, illuminating the velvet tundra around my camp.

> The secret to life is now.
> In every living moment.
> Whatever that moment may look like.

When I finally stop, look around, and see,
Actually see for the first time,
All the grace and beauty in this world,
I realize something profound.

The beauty has been here all along,
Waiting for me to get out of my head,
And into life.

Patiently the world awaits.
Waiting to celebrate our enlightenment.

When we awake, the world wakes up with us,
And the entire world is changed in an instant.

Morning.

A hummingbird buzzes into my camp, inspecting a red water bag he thinks is a flower. Sunlight blankets the green tundra, turning it to orange. Small birds bathe and wallow in a stream nearby. The stone fortress behind me steams, shimmers, and gasps as the morning sun melts away last night's frost. I fix oatmeal and green tea for breakfast, dreaming about the valleys that lie ahead. More lakes, more streams, more marshes, and ponds. More of the stunning scenery of the Mighty Winds.

How lucky am I? Free to wander at will among God's

most enchanting creations! How lucky are we? To have Wilderness! Free of charge to anyone who can walk with a backpack. The world's greatest galleries, cathedrals, monuments, and cityscapes simply cannot stand up to the heartbreaking splendor of this pristine mountain wilderness. Yet there is no one around, no one human, this side of the Divide. Wilderness calls. Heaven waits. For those simply willing to go.

A strange crash wakes me in the early dawn. Shaking the ground like thunder, it announces its close proximity. But the sound lasts too long, far too long for thunder. Fifteen seconds pass before the rumble fades back into morning silence. Then it happens again. This time more like an explosion. I crawl out of my tent to investigate, but see nothing but the fading stars of pre-dawn sky. Then I notice what happened. In a rock basin just to the north, a cloud of white dust is rising from some rubble. Rock slide. I'm humbly reminded that these mountains, like the weather, are in a state of flux, constantly changing shape, pushed up out of the ground, then weathered back down again. Always in motion. A sinuous flow.

I'm changing too. Here for just an instant. A spark of observation. The flash of a camera lens. I've been given a precious gift, the rare opportunity to capture this precise moment of beauty and perfection at this exact pinpoint in history. It's a miracle.

Like an ocean wave suspended in time, I've stepped right into the photo, and been granted an entire lifetime to explore its fine blue edges, sculpted arcs, and sensual curves. The wave will crash. This I know all too well. It will become the ocean again. But for now!

With such a rare opportunity, how can I possibly justify not seeing all there is to see? Every beach, every mountain, every river, every trail! I want to see it all. There is so much beauty. And only so much time.

> We've been given the most precious gift of all.
> This stupendous instant.
>
> This is it folks.
> The moment we've all been waiting for...

Go now. Leave your cubicle, your private office, your steady paycheck, your benefits package. What is the benefit of sitting all day inside a climate-controlled box, forty hours a week, fifty weeks a year, just to come home to another insulated box to eat, sleep, and repeat?

The real world is outside. Away from our man-made cells of concrete and steel. It's out *there*. Don't be fooled. You always have a choice. Remain part of the machine or walk away, out into the great mystery of life. Go now. Find your treasure.

I traverse a ridgeline, entering the remote Popo Agie Wilderness on the other side of the Divide. Grave Lake lies far below. The most beautiful places have some of the most dreadful names. Death Hollow. Mud Spring. Carcass Canyon. Grave Lake. The lake is two miles long, half a mile wide, and has Tahoe-blue water. Its small beaches and coves are a sight to see this far into the backcountry. If there were roads, boat ramps, and docks, this lake would be bustling with motorboats, jet skis, and barbecues. Yet Grave's appeal lies not only in her size, but also in her remoteness and inaccessibility. Twenty miles by footpath. On the far shore I pass a group of campers returning to their tents with breakfast. A stringer full of trout. I suppose a person could spend an entire summer here just fishing, camping, and relaxing at Grave Lake.

I find a spot for lunch—a round slab of granite perched twenty feet above the water. A crescent beach forms an inviting lagoon below. Rice crackers and almond butter never tasted so divine. A warm breeze brings the fragrance of spring. Buzzing dragonflies dive and dance above the water, and the peaks of the Wind Rivers dominate the horizon. A grand sensory experience. After lunch my eyes get heavy and I drift off towards an afternoon nap.

When I leave Grave Lake, the trail changes character and tests mine. The vastness of sprawling meadows, long lakes, and open tundra gives way to deep woods. My world closes off as I wind my way through dense tunnels of decaying forest, twisted tree trunks and roots, wet marshes and bogs. The air becomes eerie quiet. Just the sound of my footsteps. My labored breathing. My steady beating heart. The noises sound unnatural, out of place, like an intrusion on the silence. Everything sounds out of proportion. I think I hear a raging waterfall. A crashing in the forest. But it's just my pack brushing my shoulders, my boots on the trail, my breathing.

I struggle for traction on wet roots as I climb a steep hill. When I crest, my trail immediately descends the other side. Up. Down. Up. Going nowhere.

It's getting dark but there's nowhere to camp in this tangled mess of decaying logs and boulders. I like open spaces. Big meadows and boundless skies. Not these dark and lonely forests.

It starts to rain. Large drops pelt me in the head like insults. Then comes the lightning. It lashes out coldly, illuminating the canopy of trees above, then fades to black. I stop to put on rain gear. Another flash cracks loudly through the trees directly above my head, too close for comfort. Then darkness. More rain. The dark night of the soul.

I quicken my pace. Desperate to get out of this jungle. I'm way back inside my head, a tangled mess of thoughts bouncing all around, a downward spiral of negativity and doubt. Gray clouds compound and coalesce, then fold back in on each other, swelling like seas in a violent storm. I come to a bluff and stare up into the sky. There is something up there, something trying to get out. The clouds split open. But instead of more darkness, a patch of blue is revealed, and a single ray of light escapes. My world shifts...

> Raindrops transform into falling diamonds,
> Peaks turn to gold,
> I'm transported to a new world,
> A mystical fairyland.
>
> My thoughts freeze
> As Mother Nature whips me back
> To the present moment,
> Back into the now.

With another crescendo, my patch of blue collapses and swells back into grayness. The darkness returns, the rain continues, and the twisted forest closes in on me again. Then something flashes into my awareness—a quote.

"Judge not, lest he be judged."

I hike on. Through the rain. Through the darkness. If judgment is where my pain lies, then not only have I been judging my situation and everything around me, but I've also been judging myself. I'm actually judging myself for judging.

Ridiculous!

How much better to simply let things be as they are, and witness life with a sense of humor? It is quite silly, after all.

I hike on. Through the rain. Through the darkness. Judging the forest, judging the weather, judging my situation, judging myself. And laughing at the ridiculousness of it all.

Morning.

Sunlight, streaming through the trees, hits me squarely in the face. I camped on a small patch of grass, the only flat ground I could find last night in the darkness and the rain. I now see that I'm surrounded by a lovely grove of young aspens, glowing in the sunlight. Laying out all my clothes on the grass to do a little solar laundry, I then walk barefoot through the wet grass, down to the creek for a bath. After scrubbing away the remaining layers of yesterday's grit, I lie down on a rock to let the sun dry my freshly cleansed body. Just then a song enters my head and I start to sing...

"Gonna be a long Monday. Sittin' all alone on a mountain by a river that has no end. Gonna be a long Monday. Stuck like the tick of a clock that's come unwound."

As John Prine's lyrics sing through my head, I can't help but ponder the rest of the world at work. Today is indeed a Monday. Someone has to keep the great machine running. It will be my turn soon enough, but for now I'm grateful for my situation. My borrowed freedom. Yet difficult times lie ahead, difficult decisions will need to be made, such as do I leave this meadow, or continue to lie on this rock all day? Decisions like these trouble me so, but they are par for the course. I choose to stay. In another hour I change my mind. There is more to see, far more to see, and time is running out.

Onward. Upward. Out of the lower forest, back up onto the Continental Divide, then down through a glacier-carved passage, and into a boulder field of rocks the size of school buses.

Further down valley I meet a girl on a horse. Two more horses are in tow, loaded down with supplies: saddle bags, blankets, camping gear. This is indeed a workday for her. I learn she's working for a pack service. Her job is to deliver supplies to a group of campers down in the valley. Young, bright, beautiful—she negotiates her horse with delightful style and grace. Sharing the trail for a few minutes, we exchange stories about our adventures in the Mighty Winds. At the next junction we part ways, as she goes off to meet her party.

Soon I'm on the banks of the Little Winds River, a moment I've much been anticipating. From here I leave the main trail behind, heading off cross-country. My map shows that if I follow this river up the valley, I should reach an area called South Fork Lakes. I know that the best adventures are often off-trail, and blissful solitude will be guaranteed.

As I venture off the beaten path, the terrain grows more and more pristine. Fields of wildflowers carpet the valley floor as I march along a strip of lush green grass. After a few miles the valley opens into a sparkling lake basin.

Stopping to navigate, I see that the map refers to this area as Ranger Park. Park? I've often wondered what the mapmakers mean by park. Why park? Are there swings? Refreshments? Dancing bears and happy chipmunks? When I arrive, the description I'd jokingly imagined isn't far off.

I unstrap my pack on a patch of grass between two lakes. Behind me is a large cirque, the river valley sprawls below, and far beyond are the granite peaks of the Wind Rivers. *Cape Solitude*, as Ed Abbey would have called it. I make camp. It's only 3:00 p.m., and I've got the rest of the day to relax.

"Don't you get lonely out there all by yourself?"

The question echoes in my head. I'm always getting asked this by my family and friends, and always struggle to formulate an intelligent answer. I think about it for a moment...

When I get lonely, what's really happening? Where do I feel loneliness in my body? Is it in my stomach, my chest, my head, my toes?

Most of us never give ourselves the chance to ask these questions. At the first itch of loneliness we pick up the phone, log onto the internet, knock at the neighbor's door, or start a project. What about boredom, depression, anger, sadness? We run. Constantly we're running from our emotions. Our society is one of quick fixes. There's a pill for depression, a gadget for boredom, social media for loneliness, the pub for sadness.

We are afraid of being with our emotions. We are afraid of being with ourselves.

In college, I took a semester with an organization called Outward Bound. A three-month semester in the wilderness. I am who I am today largely because of that experience. The part of the trip I feared most was not canoeing the rapids of the Rio Grande, climbing the cliffs of Lake Superior, or backpacking through the Chihuahuan Desert. What I feared most was the three day solo. That scared me. I'd never spent more than about a half day by myself. Three days? With no one to talk to? Nothing to do? How would I survive?!

I came out of those three days knowing and understanding myself better than ever before. I'd been given the rare chance to be still with who I am, asking myself questions such as:

Who am I when I take away all my gadgets?

My friends and family?

My activities and job?

My status and gender?

My name?

Who am I???

Questions like these haunt us. Especially as we get older. Who we think we are, and who we really are, are often two very different things. Oftentimes, we believe that we are our story, everything in our lives leading up to now. We believe we are our past. But if we take away our story, our past, what's left? Searching for an answer, we pick up a spiritual book, surf the web, call up a friend. We run!

What if we just stopped? Felt the breeze on our face, the sun on our back. Focused on the lighting, the shapes, the colors.

Soon we see flowers…

Trees.

Plants.

A river.

A mountain.

The sky.

Passing clouds.

The arc of a rainbow.

Dew on a blade of grass.

Love.

Love all around.

Pure love.

Evening.

Camped in a small cluster of trees, shielded from the wind, beams of light streaming through natural windows in the canopy above. An old fire ring sits in the center of my campsite, just far enough away from the tent. It looks like it hasn't been used in years.

I tend not to make campfires in the wilderness. In pristine alpine areas unprotected from the wind and the elements, campfires are typically a bad idea. This campsite however is unique. The night is cold and windless, and rather than the typical rusty cans, melted glass, and cigarette butts that adorn the high-use fire ring, just a few blades of green grass poke through from the center of a perfectly formed rock circle. I make a small fire of seasoned pine. The incense burns clean, with almost no smoke.

It's night four. I'm mid-solo, deep in the backcountry, and far off-trail. My mind is pure, my soul is happy. I celebrate with hot chocolate.

These are the moments that make up my life. The ones I look forward to, dream about, and will look back on in the years to follow. When I'm a ninety-year-old man, with only stories left to tell, I'll reflect back on this and remember.

*That perfect fire, those pristine woods, that lake nestled
deep in the Mighty Winds. "Ah, those were the days,"
I'll say. "Young and free. Alive with dreams as big as
the world. What I wouldn't give to go back there..."*

Then in an instant. Like magic! HERE I AM. Right
back in those woods, by the lake, beside the fire. The old
man gets his wish yet again.

I know of no better way to live my life than from the
perspective of that old man. The ninety-year-old me.
Because I always know what he would say. And it's never, "I should have worked more, saved more, bought a
nicer car, a bigger house, been more responsible."

So we sit, late into the night, just me and myself.
Getting to know each other better. Sipping tea, stoking
the fire, high on life. High in the Mighty Winds.

> I'm the luckiest man alive.
> I've walked the rooftops of the world,
> Tasted the sweetest of mountain water,
> Found God in a desert canyon,
> And married a beautiful girl who loves me.
> All of this in just forty years.

3:30 a.m.
I get up to pee. Ten shooting stars pass by in the time it

takes to relieve myself; one leaves a trail streaking across the entire Milky Way. There is no moon, but starlight illuminates the walls of the basin, creating a star-filled fortress. Of all the places I've ever been, surely this must be the clearest, darkest night sky I've ever witnessed.

I walk out to the water's edge, gazing out across the jet-black surface. Stars on the water. Stars in the sky. I turn back around to face my camp. It flickers and glows in the firelight. I etch the image into my memory banks the best I can, for future reflection. Then, chuckling at the dreaminess of it all, I imagine a circle of bears dancing around the fire.

In the north sky appears the Big Dipper, then the Pleiades, two constellations that have always been there for me, keeping me company, watching over me, guiding me along on my journeys. Sending my love and gratitude, I thank them for this life, rich with leisure and abundance. I have two more days in the wilderness—I shall not take a single moment for granted.

Morning.

Everything is completely still. The lake acts as a giant mirror, reflecting the jagged peaks, the blue sky, the puffy clouds overhead. Small spruce trees, six to eight feet tall, line the water's edge. They are symmetrically perfect, an astounding fact given that snow covers them completely in the winter. Preserved in the fine crystals of Rocky Mountain powder, they somehow manage to retain their flawless shape. A fragile balance of harshness and beauty.

I stare out over the water, as two ducks from opposite ends of the lake paddle towards one another. They meet in the center, then continue side by side, across the glassy surface, with no apparent agenda, no hurry, no destination in mind. Just a peaceful morning paddle. My heart aches for Valerie, my wife, my one true love, back in Boulder, patiently awaiting my return. In two days I get to see her.

Clouds fill the basin and it starts to rain.

I quickly make breakfast, break down camp, and lace up my boots. Today's route is off-trail, up over a ridge, across the Divide, and then back down, connecting to the Lizard Head Trail on the other side. Maybe. The connection may not be possible, but that's what makes an adventure an adventure.

I start my climb in the rain, sloshing through wet marshes, picking my way through slippery boulder fields. I reach my ridge by noon, just as the rain lets up. Stepping out to the edge, I peer over the ridge, but my excitement is short-lived. Instead of my route I find a thousand-foot drop, straight off a cliff. Impassable.

The majestic Cirque of the Towers lies on the other side of the ridge, a world-renowned climbing destination, a beautiful sight to behold. But while taking in the majesty, I must grasp the reality of my situation. This is a dead end.

I consult the map for options. I could hike back to camp, 2,000 feet of backtracking to square one. Or I could try traversing this ridge. The spine is narrow but it looks walkable. It could lead over to the next basin. My map shows it dropping down to a group of lakes labeled *Shadow Lake Basin*. The route is completely uncertain of course, requiring both ascending and descending over large boulders, scree fields, wet talus. But I'll be moving forward.

I decide to give it a shot. If things get too dangerous I'll simply head back the way I came. Besides, it's all dangerous to some degree. Backpacking is dangerous. Solo is dangerous. Hell, driving here is dangerous. But there is a point where the risk outweighs the gain, and I'm pretty good at knowing where that point is.

Less than an hour later I manage to traverse the ridge, over to the other side of the cirque. With fingers crossed I again peer over. Another drop. Sketchy to be sure. But doable. There are cracks in the rock, ledges, places where I can lower my pack with a rope, climb down. The alpine lake basin is there, right where the map said it would be, and she's gorgeous. Three lakes, all in a row, all emerald green. I can already pick out my campsite in a grove of pines, 2,000 feet below.

I scramble down the rock, lowering my pack with rope in a few places, but with relative ease I'm back on stable

ground in less than an hour. In my final steps to the basin floor I marvel over my feat. Failure to success, adver-
sity to possibility, a dead-end to a mere detour. After a
day of uncertainty I've accomplished my goal.

Strolling beside the sparkling lakes, my feet rejoic-
ing on flat ground once again, every song with the word
Celebration bursts through my mind. You know which
songs those are, the cheesiest ones! Singing my way back
to camp, the feeling of victory blooms in my chest. What
a grand entrance to my last night in the wilderness.
Dropping down from the sky, over a ridge, that even as
I gaze back up now looks impassible, and down into this
pristine lake basin.

It's amazing what pops into my head at the end of a
really good trip. Grand thoughts. Memories of childhood,
family Thanksgivings, old friends, friends who have
passed away, and ones I haven't talked to in decades. My
life flashes before my eyes. All of it. Every little blessed
detail. And it's all quite beautiful. I've come to call this
moment a *Life Celebration*. Something only a peak experience can provide. It's a feeling of pure ecstasy. A high
as high as I'll ever know.

CHAPTER SEVEN

Capitol Reef, Utah

THINK IT'S COLD, but who would know? The air is so still, temperature cannot be felt. Then there's this silence, screaming into my ears. There's no escape. I drop something on the rock beside me, to break the silence, my spoon. The screaming ceases. Then nothing.

A slight breeze from some far-off place stings my face. Yes. It's cold. With the breeze comes the hollow sound of the night, darkness, cold, winter.

The tenth of November. My pen moves all by itself, across the paper, recording the moment, the great mystery. I'm trying hard to keep up. The facts, man. Nothing but the facts. The truth for God's sake! But what's the truth?

The breeze returns, reminding me of the night, the desert, the cold moon, my warm sleeping bag. I climb in and dream of twisting canyons, petroglyphs, cliff dwellings, hidden water.

Morning.

The sun rises behind me, not far from where it set last night, in the south. Shadows creep slowly across the land, revealing labyrinths, chambers, alcoves, chasms. Hot coffee steams from my mug. I check my thermometer. Nineteen degrees.

Chunks of lava litter my sandstone slab of a campsite. To the north are enormous blobs of rock—orange, cream, red—sculpted by wind, water, and time. They tower above me like stone gods standing watch. The rock is quilted, not cracked and broken, but folded and creased, like the patterns of an old blanket. Hoodoos guard the perimeter, marching tall against dark blue sky. Gargoyles. Goblins. Jabba-the-Huts. Witnessing the passing of time. Days. Years. Centuries. They too will wear away. Their forms constantly changing, telling their own story. They look like old faces, wise ancestors. Telling the story of time. Unfathomable time. We all have a story to tell. Here it is laid out like an open book. Take a walk out onto these rocks, and the story unfolds in high-definition color and startling clarity. It's a walk through time.

I've been here before. On my way to Glen Canyon, Escalante, Pariah. A land of twisting sandstone, hidden rivers, dripping springs, cactus, pinyons, junipers, cottonwoods, lizards, frogs, ravens, scorpions, vultures.

This place beckons me. Tugging at my soul over the hundreds of miles of desert, prairie, mountain, rock. Like heroin. Alluring. Seducing. Distracting me from my work. Haunting my dreams.

What is it about this place? What is it about this desert?

I search for an answer but come up dry, like always. There is something here beyond words. Something unexplainable. A presence. Something living, breathing. Listening.

This place *is* time. Witnessing the rain, the wind, freezing and thawing. A canvas on which the Earth paints its story, leaping from the landscape, saturating the senses, invoking the wildest of imaginations. Art without the artist. Painting without the painter. Beauty for the sake of beauty. The work of God.

I walk gently onto the canvas, beginning to feel myself part of the piece. I'm here—not to dig and drill, excavate and haul away, probe and prod, measure and examine, rape and pillage, tame and conquer—but to witness. To be in the presence of Greatness.

I want to listen,
Not to the desert,
But along with her.

I want to see,
Not only the rocks,
But to see what they see.

I want to experience,
Not just the beauty,
But to become it myself.

Slipping into the mouth of Pleasant Creek Canyon, I'm at once drawn into the mystery. Carvings of bighorn sheep, antelope, snakes, spirals, men with horns and spears, handprints. A thousand years old? Two thousand? They weave together a story. A time before words, before dates, before time itself.

Further down-canyon I find other carvings:

EMUFORD, APRIL 21, 1907.
CHESALT, SEPT 29, 1933.

A story of progress. Time. Evolution. They all seem to be saying the same thing:

I WAS HERE.

Around every corner I flip another page in Earth's life-sized history book. I resist the urge to make my own mark; ours is already large enough. Strewn about the canyon floor are more lava chunks, jet-black against bleached stone. They tell yet another story: A time before man.

My mind wanders to the cliff dwellers. They chose this place. I can feel their energy emanating from the ruins, the paintings, the walls. Living high in these cliffs— a room with a view—they must have felt protected, safe from weather, predators, other tribes. With water and abundant idle time, I picture them making love on the sandstone, crafting fine pottery, gathering water, preparing meals. Day in. Day out. Watching over the rocks. Soaking up the great power. The energy. The silence. Then birthing their children with no hospitals or doctors. There may have been medicine men, shamans, masters of the trade, traveling the canyons, trading their services for a meal, a clay pot, precious stones. Or just appeasing the gods, serving mankind.

Evidence suggests war, violence. But in the long gaps between, I imagine a peaceful, spiritual people with respect for the land, the water they drink, the animals they hunt, the shelter the rock provides. Enlightened beings? Perhaps. I envision them wise, happy, full of gratitude and love for this land of undeniable beauty.

I scramble up the side of a ravine, kicking footholds into crumbling rock and loose sand, climbing out of my canyon and up onto a foundation of unbroken stone. Waterpocket Fold is my objective, an island in the sky of continuous rock stretching out for miles—rippled, folded, polished, eroded in such a way that it holds hundreds of water pockets, tinajas, or *tanks* as the Park Service likes to call them. They hold thousands of gallons of rainwater.

Waterpocket Fold *should* be devoid of water entirely. It's far from the creeks, streams, and seeps that lie in the canyons below. However, when it rains, water runs through eroded channels in the rock, carving away layers of stone over eons of time. The water has formed holes the size of bathtubs and child-sized swimming pools.

Tinajas are common. They can be primary sources of drinking water on a long journey across the desert. But they're elusive, often revealing themselves at the most crucial of moments, water bottle running dry, mouth hot and sandy, the lingering threat of a headache. Only then do they appear like sparkling jewels deep inside a shady pocket, as precious as life itself.

I've camped close to these tinajas. Many are quite small—often no more than a few inches deep, a foot or two long. Strangely, I've extracted gallon after gallon from these tiny pools, the water line barely changing, as if the water were coming up from the ground.

In Waterpocket Fold tinajas are everywhere. Some hold thousands of gallons of rainwater. The abundance seems absurd, exceedingly extravagant. Some have grown their own gardens—reeds, flowers, trees up to twenty feet tall—all against a landscape of bare, naked rock, sprawling for acres, until the horizon drops off into space. Like tropical islands in a sea of sand and stone.

I stop to peer into a tinaja, tucked into a crack between two boulders. There is life: water bugs, striders, frogs, butterflies, mosquitoes, bees. They all, somehow, live here. Of all the creeks, lakes, rivers, and ponds of the world, these organisms live here, high above the desert floor, in Waterpocket Fold. How did they end up here? How did the cliff dwellers? How did I?

Camp.

I stare at a low moon and it looks animated. Absurdly huge and yellow, like a child's drawing, against the silhouetted cliffs. The Big Dipper appears, also larger than life, taking up half the sky. Rocks glow in the moonlight and I feel embraced, wrapped up in the essence of love itself, held tightly in her healing hands. I offer my love back: to the Wilderness, the desert, the tinajas, the rocks, the sun, the moon and the stars, and to Mother Earth. After all we've taken, her love is still stronger than ever.

Beyond all else we must remember who we are, where we come from, and where we will return. There comes a time when we must make our pilgrimage. Leave our houses, our cities of concrete and steel, and make our journey back to Wilderness. Back home, to the way it was, and still is, in places like Capitol Reef National Park.

National Park. This I must keep reminding myself. Our parks serve a great purpose, not just for preservation, but also as a funnel. The Designated Route. Mobs of tourists, RVs, buses, and family station wagons out on summer vacation need a place to go. Our national parks serve this purpose, complete with entrance fees, advance reservation campgrounds, snack bars, game rooms, bowling alleys, roped-off viewpoints, paved trails, lodges, and reserved backcountry campsites. Permit required. For a fee.

Our national parks are a one-stop-shop for the enjoyment of all ages and skill levels. Our national treasure. How else could the masses enjoy all that America has to offer, all crammed in a one-week vacation? The national parks inspire, educate, and impress upon their visitors that wilderness is worth protecting, for future generations to come. A vital role.

But they are not for everyone.

Certainly not for folks of my kind, who tend to drive out late after work on a Friday night, spur-of-the-moment, underprepared, half-planned, half-assed, wide-eyed, driving through the night coffee-buzzed, sleep-deprived, arriving late (after-hours), without reservation (no permit), craving solitude, salvation, and a private paradise at the edge of the world. And most of all...

We want to be alone!

Capitol Reef is different. There are few trails, few (official) scenic viewpoints, one small campground, and no designated backcountry sites. A backcountry permit is required, and you can get one at the visitor center. For free.

"Where do you plan to hike?" the ranger lady asks me.

She looks frazzled. She hadn't been expecting visitors. Not on a weekday.

I'm also frazzled, fumbling through maps, printouts from the internet, notes scribbled on the back of junk mail envelopes.

"Umm..."

"Well, what *trail* will you be hiking?" she finally asks me.

I'm not used to this kind of interrogation. Not while on vacation.

"I plan to start at Spring Creek. No. Pleasant Creek," I tell her, slightly apprehensive to reveal my route, or lack thereof.

"And from *there*?" she asks.

"Then up to the Waterpocket Fold, and hopefully down to Capitol Gorge. But maybe not. I'll be off-trail. It will depend on the route, my mood, *you know*—the scenery, my map skills, the weather..." I trail off, glancing up to see if she understands. If she *gets* me.

She scribbles something down on my permit and sends me off into the desert. My kind of park ranger! My kind of National Park. And one of the least-visited in the US. Probably it will stay that way. After all, who really wants to drive all the way out into the middle of nowhere, just for a few short trails and a tiny campground? NO SERVICES.

~

Afternoon.

Clear skies overhead. Slight breeze from the south. Abundant sunshine. Eighty degrees.

This place is as beautiful as Arches, spectacular as Canyonlands, monumental as Zion, curious as Bryce, yet with no people. In two days I've seen not a trace nor a footprint, aside from my own. Must have gotten turned around again.

I indulge in an afternoon nap, dreaming of Mexico and buckets of iced Coronas.

~

Morning.

I'm awakened to clouds the color of cotton candy. Wrapped in my sleeping bag, I reach over to light my stove, starting water for coffee. Like chameleons, the canyon walls begin to take on the color of the clouds, covering my camp in rosy pink. When the water has boiled I add the coffee grounds straight to the pot. Cowboy coffee, best kind. Inhaling the aroma I sit back and listen: My cook stove ticks, my belly rumbles, and beautiful, blissful, blessed nothingness.

The stillness in these waterless canyons just before sunrise, surely must be the thickest, most profound form of silence on Earth. There is nothing but nothing. Careful not to move I soak in the great power, for even the slightest bit of sound could break the spell. It's all so effortless, so simple, so sweet, so pure.

What is all this *doing* all the time? What is all this *running around*? What are we trying to achieve? What's the purpose of all of it? Peace? Happiness? Fulfillment? Recognition? I search but again words fail. Just nothing. Not even a raven to consult this cold November morning. I look to the junipers...

"You're asking this again?" they say. "You still don't get it?"

The clouds turn gray, rolling towards the sun. Smells of winter. Cold.

Not even a bug or lizard. They're all in cocoons, pods, underground tunnels, sleeping away the winter. Just this curious fellow in the bright orange sleeping bag. What is he doing? Walking these desert canyons, carrying his heavy load, asking junipers for answers. Who's this guy? Who is he?

"Who is who?"

The words escape my mouth with a hollow sound, ricocheting from wall to wall, down-canyon, off into the abyss. Then I disappear.

There is nothing left,
But all of eternity.

I understand now.
I understand it all.

I remember what it is,
That I always forget.

They say that wisdom comes with age. So who could be wiser than the sky, with its eternal sunsets, thunderstorms, stars, galaxies? Who could be wiser than the rocks, these monoliths of stone, witness to all, over the eons of time?

There's an all-knowingness out here. It lies within all this silence and stillness. A wisdom so profound that it transcends words. An understanding so pure it cannot be explained, cannot be taught, nor grasped by the human mind. Only felt. Experienced firsthand.

When I tap into this wisdom, a switch is flipped, a reversal happens. My mind, always up front, driving and controlling everything, takes a back seat. And my soul, hiding quietly in the back seat, jumps up to take shotgun.

Like a domesticated wolf returned to the wild, a spark of energy rekindles my true nature. I remember, pause for a moment, then go bounding off into the wild. Never to look back.

My pen moves all by itself. Across the paper, recording the moment, the great mystery. I'm trying hard to keep up. The facts, man. Nothing but the facts. The truth!

With a trembling hand and a tear in my eye I now know. I finally understand.

The Truth is who I am.

CHAPTER EIGHT

Set Sail to the Open Sea of Life

WHAT WOULD YOU DO if you were given a hundred thousand dollars? In your answer lies *your dream.*

Well, maybe.

This was just a game. Valerie and I were hanging with some friends one cold December evening in our mountain house. Huddled around the fire, we drank Syrah and toyed with the question. A hundred thousand dollars is an interesting figure. Not enough for most folks to retire on, yet enough to do something big. But what?

When it was my turn, the answer came quickly. Travel. Valerie winked back at me, her blue eyes twinkling in the firelight, appearing to be in agreement. But wait, the game is not so easy. Details, details, our friends insisted. Travel where? By what mode? For how long and for what purpose? Someone refilled my wine glass as I thought about it some more.

There are so many choices. How to decide? Patagonia? Chile? Spain? Italy? Someone retrieved chocolate ice cream from the freezer and passed bowls around. I kept going... British Columbia? Alaska? Mexico? French Polynesia? The Maldives? I could've gone all night. Morocco? South Africa? Vietnam? Our planet is incredible. I'd like to see it all, but where to begin?

"What about America?" someone said. I thought about it for a moment. I live here and haven't seen but a fraction of my own continent. There are places within a day's drive that I've never even explored. Our country is the most diverse of them all. We have mountains, beaches, canyons, rainforests, rivers, lakes, creeks, lagoons, caves! It's all right here, in my own backyard, more than I could see in a lifetime. Just hop in the car, turn the key, and go.

The nice thing about America is you can follow the weather. Hit the high country in summer, deserts and beaches in the winter. We could migrate. Like birds. Like nomads.

Yes! I would explore the American West.

Fast forward six months. No one has given us a hundred thousand dollars. Not yet anyhow. But Valerie and I both quit our jobs, sold our house, moved into a truck camper, and paid off all our debt with the proceeds from the house sale. We have enough money left over to live modestly on the road for a year, or longer. The exercise worked. If our dream is to travel the American West, then we shall follow that dream!

We've taken the leap, interrupted our routine, set sail into the open sea of life. Into the mystic. With the flip of a switch our life has transformed into an adventure, our future unwritten, each day a spontaneous fulfillment of desire.

There *is* a plan, to be sure. A rough layout of sorts—trails highlighted on maps, notes scribbled on paper, guidebooks earmarked—but it's loose, everything is subject to change. It all depends on our moods, the weather, the scenery, *you know*...

It's an open-ended journey, no definitive timeline. A year? Longer? Who knows? Life is not certain, so why live like it is?

For now it's life on the road. Kayaks, mountain bikes, backpacking gear, maps, guidebooks, clothes and food—everything is neatly stored and stowed away in our little house on wheels. Chuggin' down the highway, in pursuit of beauty, love, and the American Dream.

CHAPTER NINE

Rabbit Valley, Utah

A SONIC WIND BLASTS the hot July desert. We're in Utah, and the daytime heat is a stifling 100 degrees. But the nights are pleasant, invoking deep sleep, and long, exotic desert dreams.

A symphony of scents and subtle sounds has the grasses—now golden in the heat of the sun—in a constant dance. A fly buzzes my ear, sounding like a lawnmower, grinding the desert silence to a halt, if only for a split second. Then nothing but the dry wind. The crackling heat.

To the southwest, the La Sal Mountains tower above blood-colored cliffs—the spires and ridges of Moab,

Arches, and Canyonlands. Snow clings to the peaks, stark and brilliant in the morning sun. The desert stretches out before me: Knowles Canyon, Mee Canyon, Dark Canyon, Grand Gulch, Indian Creek, The Colorado River, Lake Powell. Beyond that, the Grand Canyon, Painted Desert, Sycamore Canyon, The Superstitions, Cabeza Prieta. Further still, an immeasurable expanse of nameless gullies, slots, wrinkles, labyrinths, winding canyons, and cathedrals of stone.

Like Medusa she seduces me. Provocative shapes and colors, tempting me out onto the desert rock, the sizzling stone, the crackling dirt, the hot silence. Tempting death. Promising Eden. The Holy Grail. The Hanging Garden. Hidden Water. The oasis in the lost city of stone, on the fringes of society, far from industry, developments, progress. It's out there. I just know it. I've been there before.

A raven buzzes close, riding the thermals, six hundred feet above the canyon floor. Yet on this ridge we are at eye level. With two squawks of disapproval he reminds me that it's not my time. Not yet. The desert will wait, as she always does. I'll return perhaps in late winter, or early spring, when temperatures are more suitable for survival. Our current destination lies somewhere to the north. The Wasatch, the Sawtooths, the Cascades, the Pacific Northwest. It will be cooler up there. The desert will wait as she always does. So patiently.

CHAPTER TEN

The High Uintas, Utah

How I got here,
I cannot recall.

There was one reality,
Now here is another.

Memories flash through my head,
From some other world.

A child in a plastic kiddie pool,
A teen at a high school dance,
A businessman wearing a tie.

I try to piece together the details,
Build some sort of timeline,
Tell the story.

The story?
It unravels in my fingers.

The hand of time ticks.
I hold tightly to the needle,
I don't want to miss an instant.
That is where it all happens.

CHAPTER ELEVEN

Sawtooth Wilderness, Idaho

A FULL MOON RISES over El Capitan, the stone monolith dominating the view through our tent door. The roar of whitewater engulfs us, cascading through a surprise valley of jagged peaks and steep canyons. I've dreamt about this place. Spent hours marveling over its vastness, collecting maps, guidebooks, magazine articles. It's the largest concentration of roadless land in the lower forty-eight states.

Idaho is mostly Wilderness. Public land. Owned by Americans. All Americans. It's your land. As it is mine. 4,795,782 acres to be exact. It's about time I go see my land.

We are backpacking the Sawtooth Wilderness. Adjacent lies the Selway-Bitterroot Wilderness. Adjacent to that lies the Frank Church River of No Return Wilderness. Four million acres in total. There's only one way to experience it: on foot, with a backpack. For the next several weeks Valerie and I will be doing just that.

Our hike starts in a dead forest. Lodgepole pines killed by the pine beetle, then burned by fires. Valerie moves quickly, head down, gaining elevation fast. I'm anxious too, eager to find higher ground, away from all this death and decay. In a few miles the dead pines give way to lush groundcover, dank soil, colorful wildflowers, charming mushrooms. Trees come to life, waterfalls erupt from rocky ravines, we wade through deep streams, the water frigid yet crystal clear.

Morning.

We wake to an illuminated basin drenched in soft sunlight. We fix breakfast and hit the trail early, intending to climb three passes before lunch, avoiding the afternoon storms. We hope to make it to some alpine lakes, where we'll camp, swim, and nap away the rest of the afternoon.

This is the first trek of our year-long journey and quickly I relax into the routine. Cooking, cleaning, setting up and breaking down camp. I enjoy the simplicity, the slower pace, and living outside.

I can feel it happening already. True magic does exist. It just remains hidden, not in the far reaches of our imagination, but right here on Earth, tucked into the deep valleys, the rugged mountain ranges, and the far reaches of this planet. Revealing itself only to those who are willing to walk and make the journey.

The brisk morning air has us light on our feet. I follow Valerie up the trail, thinking of others who walked here before. The ones who built the trails, fought for wilderness designation, and dedicated their lives to the protection of this land, so that future generations can also experience this magic. Unspoiled beauty like this remains rare, sacred.

These pristine places of magic and beauty, they are not exclusive. They are not here solely for the rich and famous, the royal and the privileged few. They are here for everyone, free of charge.

I'd take comfort in that.

No matter how bad your life can ever get, how low you can feel, how much society lets you down, you can always come back here. You can always go home.

You can lose everything, but no one can take away your Wilderness. She's always here. Waiting. Ready to welcome you back with open arms. Ready to welcome you home.

I don't know what happens when we die, but I imagine it must be something of a coming home. Fortunately, we don't have to die to experience this. There is heaven right here. Right here on Earth. Come on in, see for yourself.

Hop in a car, hitch a ride, or simply start walking. Just get here! You will be cleansed, you will be renewed, and be given a new perspective on life. A fresh start. Ready for the next chapter, born again into the world. Yes! Wilderness can do all of that!

We crest our first pass, and I can't help but wonder how these areas retain their astounding beauty and perfection throughout the ages. It's as if they've been placed under a secret dome of protection, somehow immune to the devastation of progress. The world changes, yet their timelessness remains. I know that change *is* happening, massive change, yet here time seems to stand still.

Our cellphones have no service, our cash and credit cards are useless, the past has no relevance, and schedules melt away. Our breathing becomes full, our digestive systems regular, our eyes begin to sparkle, our facial muscles relax. Our minds, plagued with the curse of incessant thought, fall into a blissful state of peace.

Gliding down the trail we begin to see—really see— the life, beauty, and love that surrounds us. Our stale and cold world of details begins to dissolve into new energy and warmth. We realize that the world is not against us, but here to support us, love us, and guide us along.

We've just been too busy thinking. Always thinking. Lost inside ourselves and our thoughts. Too far gone to realize that what we seek, what we long for, is already here. We just needed to lose the baggage, put down the gadgets, and take a long walk. Open our eyes to the wonder and unspeakable beauty that is Life.

"Life moves pretty fast. If you don't stop and look around once and a while, you could miss it."
– Ferris Bueller

CHAPTER TWELVE

Boise National Forest, Idaho

HOME IS WHERE YOU PARK IT.
We live in a country that allows us to travel freely through National Forest land, following any number of dirt roads and trails to our own slice of paradise, for the day, night, or week. Up to sixteen days in one area, says the National Forest sign. Free of charge. It's yours! Just by being a US citizen.

The sun drops behind the Boise mountains as we pull off onto Forest Road 594, somewhere south of Lowman. Valerie holds the map and I drive, negotiating our little camper through creeks, rocks, potholes. Higher and higher we climb up a one-lane dirt road, until we spot a clearing high up on a ridge. This will be our home for the night. I pull in and shut off the engine. Silence floods through the windows of our Chevy pickup, and for a moment we just sit and take in the stillness. I open the door and step out onto the dirt while Valerie pulls a couple of cold beers from the ice chest. In the dark, we walk along the old two-track road for a while, holding hands, sipping beers, watching shooting stars, listening to the songs of crickets. Our sleep is long and deep, full of infinite dreams.

Morning wakes us to the sounds of birdsong. I peek outside and see rays of sunlight beaming through lush old-growth forest. There are no cars, no planes, no other sounds whatsoever. Nothing but the morning.

It's incredible to wake this way. Each day in a new place. Each day fresh, full of wonder, full of possibility. I make coffee and we take a morning stroll down the dusty old road. Like an image from a painting, it's narrow, smooth, and lined with pine needles. All around are summer wildflowers—yellow, red, orange, pink, purple. Oh how I'd like to know their names, if only I could remember that plant and flower guide.

This morning air! Soft. Like a cotton sheet on a cool summer night.

Further down the road we're led to views sprawling across the hillsides and ridges of the Boise National

Forest. It all reminds me of my youth, trips to Tennessee, North Carolina, and the Blue Ridge Mountains. The forest is deep, lush, vibrant, healthy. Buzzing with life. The leaves on the trees sparkle as they catch the light of the morning sun. Inhaling the crisp air, I breathe in the fragrance of pure summer.

When the sun creeps over the horizon we return to camp. Valerie retreats to the camper to prepare breakfast and I sit outside for a while, observing the small community we've stumbled upon. Butterflies dance around in circles, chasing one another like children playing in a park. Flies buzz around in their busy desperation. Finches and Steller's jays dart here and there, calling to one other from their various perches on tree branches. Not a care in the world do they seem to have this incredibly fine morning.

A hummingbird flies close, inspecting my orange coffee mug. He hovers for a moment, giving me a curious look, then zooms off. An elk dashes through the thick woods, mysterious and dark, half-hidden, moving without a sound. Chipmunks scurry through the grass, they seem to be having the most fun of all, chasing, playing, celebrating the day. Rather than hunt they seem to stumble upon their food, as if tripping over it by accident. With a twitch they grab a nut, hold it in their paws, eat it like an apple, then drop it on the ground partially eaten, resuming their game of chase.

Smells of bacon, sizzling eggs, fresh coffee...

CHAPTER THIRTEEN

Mount Jefferson Wilderness, Oregon

RIGHT AWAY I REALIZE I've made the right decision—to start my hike from here. I'd intended to drop Valerie off at the Breitenbush Hot Springs Resort to soak and relax for a few days, then drive several miles up the road to the trailhead to begin my trip. But when we relayed our plans to the front desk attendant, I was surprised to learn that there is a trail leading into the wilderness from here. The idea of starting and ending my trip at the hot springs sounded too good to pass up.

I get Valerie checked in to her cabin, grab my pack, then we both head down a narrow forest trail to some hot springs by the river. Stripping out of our clothes, we enter the water for a soak. Valerie's rosy skin goosebumps in the cool mountain air, and immediately I regret my decision to go hiking without her. But we've been traveling together nonstop, living inside a tiny camper. I want to go exploring, but she needs the relaxation. The time apart will be healthy for us both. We linger in the hot springs for as long as possible, then kiss one last time as she wishes me a great trip and a safe return. We part ways and I start my trek, up a faint trail, through old-growth timber, into the jungle of the Willamette National Forest.

In no time the forest explodes with color, wild beyond imagination. At this low elevation the canopy is impossibly green, dripping with lush ferns and thick rhododendron. Hemlocks are eight feet around, giant cedars are hundreds of years old. Oh the stories they could tell! Then there's the Breitenbush River, wide, meandering, so clear that I can see every rock, every fish, every log beneath its surface. I walk on pine needles, layers upon layers of them, so thick that the ground feels like carpet. When I walk there is no sound.

Moving quickly is completely out of the question. Not here. Better to wander, stroll, creep my way through, taking in every little detail. Three-dimensional spider webs, moss and lichens, salamanders and tree frogs, mushrooms and berries. I will not go hungry—around every corner there are blackberries, raspberries, huckleberries.

To hike quickly here would be like racing through an art gallery. What could possibly lie ahead that would be more beautiful, more abundant, more pristine than this old-growth rainforest where I now stand? I slow my stride to a crawl, relaxing into the surreal landscape, losing myself in the sights, the sounds, the shapes, and textures. I'm wide open and alert, as I wander through the mystical Oregon Wilderness.

The boundaries between life and death have grown blurry. I can no longer tell the difference. An ancient tree stump is covered in moss, ferns grow out from the top. A downed log is blanketed in tiny pink flowers. Even the ground is alive, thick with spongy green plant life. Mushrooms grow everywhere, and out of everything. Rocks are covered in fuzzy botanical gardens of their own, appearing as mounds of organic life.

Unlike the desert, where life is spaced widely apart, here everything is intertwined. Plants grow out of plants, trees grow out of trees, yet rather than competition, I see community. Symbiotic relationships. Life enabling life. Never before has the circle of life been so perfectly laid out before my eyes. There is no beginning, no end. No life, no death. Just a natural flow. Rather than a thousand species, I see one. Earth Species.

Where does one organism stop and another begin? What is what, and where do we draw the line? How to make a separation? Without one we cannot have the other.

Without the decay, we cannot have new birth. A tree falls, crumbling to soil, nourishing ferns, lichens, and mushrooms. These provide food for ants, beetles, tree frogs, salamanders. In turn, they provide food for owls, hawks, mountain lions, bears. They too die, feeding the vultures and ravens. Finally worms turn their remains back to soil as the cycle repeats itself, over and over. So is the circle of life.

In our cities of concrete and steel, we've removed ourselves from these cycles. We've forgotten the circle of life and the interconnectedness of all things. A shift in consciousness is all that is required. Life is abundant, with plenty to go around, until things fall out of balance. We will either evolve, or we will die.

I climb into a deep gorge, and realize that I'm sweating profusely. With rainforests come humidity, and my T-shirt is soaked, my hat dripping. As a matter of fact, I am drenched from head to toe. Not since my early days in the forests of the Midwest have I perspired like this. How different are the humid forests of the Cascades from the arid pines of the Rockies. I dunk my head at a stream crossing to cool off, but the relief is short-lived. Within minutes I'm dripping sweat again. Surprisingly though, my energy is high, very high as a matter of fact, despite the heat. Oxygen is the advantage here. Lots of it. In Colorado I'm typically hiking above 10,000 feet, here I'm barely above two thousand. My blood is rich as oxygen surges through my veins. I'm exuberant, despite the fountain of sweat pouring from the top of my head.

Day two.

Thunder rumbles, but the rain never comes. In the warmth and humidity of the night, I sleep on top of my bag rather than in it. Now Mount Jefferson greets me in the blazing morning light. Crawling from my tent, I start coffee, fry some potatoes and bacon. Ah to be backpacking! Alone again with wilderness!

We are social creatures. Surrounding ourselves with constant relationships, we often neglect one of the most important. The relationship with ourselves. The first realization on a solo trek is the most obvious. You are alone. This can be scary. Especially if you share each and every day with a significant other. But patience is a virtue. Just wait, give it a little time, soon you'll start to rekindle that quiet relationship with yourself, the one you began long ago, when you ventured out into a completely new world, full of wonder and possibility.

Like magic, you'll feel a twitch—that same sparkle you had as a child. The one you see in an infant's eyes, the one you had before you were born, and the one you'll take with you when you die. It's still there. It never goes away.

Wilderness can do this. But you must go it alone. It's a journey, and not an easy one at first, but if you can tap into your true essence, even if for a moment, it is worth it. You start to feel a new sense of freedom, the playfulness of a child. The day is yours. Yours alone. You can do anything! What a joy it is to simply be alive, healthy, human, here.

With a deep breath of pure mountain air, you smile in gratitude, heading out into your day of adventure. You've stepped out of your routine, out of your story. Now you are creating. Your book is unwritten; you create the story, minute-by-minute, frame-by-frame, second-by-second.

The best part? Returning back home after your trek is over. Walking through the door with that crazed look of pure ecstasy on your face as your spouse says, "What the hell did you do out there?" You smile and laugh it off, giving them a big hug because you are back. YOU are back.

Day three.

I start my hike late. Today is pretty open, all the days are open. There are no schedules, no deadlines, no to-do lists. So are itineraries in the high country. The *high* country. The contrast from yesterday's rainforest to this alpine tundra is astonishing. A rare treat to see such progression—like witnessing the entire state of Oregon in a single hike. From an elevation of 2,400 to 6,800 feet, I've encountered almost every type of terrain.

On top of the world, dense forest has given way to fields of wildflowers, winding streams, and views in all directions. Entire mountain ranges unravel before me.

Mount Washington is a constant backdrop. Rising from this place of unimaginable beauty to an elevation of 10,500 feet, with gleaming white glaciers clinging to her highest peaks. To reach the summit would require another 3,700 feet of climbing on loose rock, ice, and snow. I think I'll stay down here, in Eden. I don't need to see God just yet.

Day four.

I awake in the sparkling paradise of Jefferson Park. The rain finally came last night, unleashed from the heavens, covering the ground in an inch of hail. The skies are now blue and washed clean. On trail by 11:00 a.m., an early start by my standards, I descend from this lovely park down into a dark, shaded forest. The shade is welcome, and soon I'm back into a jungle of lush fern and rhododendron.

I've switched worlds. Dark forests make me lonely, leaving me longing for a meadow, a mountain, a lake or a view. But these forests are different. Soon I'm munching on huckleberries and blackberries, ripe and plentiful along the side of the trail. At a creek crossing, I take a much-needed bath, have some lunch, and nap by the stream. When I wake, my first thought is to stay here for the rest of the afternoon. But it's only three o'clock, and there's much too much day left for exploring. So I descend back into dark botanical forest. Hours pass before I emerge from the jungle, my senses overwhelmed, my body tired, my mind spent. I'm ready to camp. At the first flat spot I see, I stop, pitch my tent, and crawl inside for a nap. Second nap of the day, much deserved, much needed.

If we slowed our lives down enough to allow for naps, wouldn't we all have more enjoyable days, more productive days? Why do our work ethics tells us to work more? Work harder? Work longer? Anything less than eight hours—unacceptable. Towards the end of our workday, how productive are we, really? Are we actually working at that point, or just staring at a computer screen, staring at the clock? Passing the time?

What happened to working smarter? Why not focus on production instead of hours? With all the advancements in technology and science over the past twenty years, why do we still need eight hours a day, forty hours a week, to get the job done? You'd think we'd be down to about an hour and a half. Now that's progress. That's evolution!

But NO! That is not the way the world works. This country is based on growth. More production, growth for the sake of growth. Like the cancer cell. Until we evolve and leave the anthill mentality of work for the sake of work behind, have we really evolved at all? WORK LESS, PLAY MORE. It's not just evolution, it's revolution. Progress!

Waking from nap number two, I climb out of my tent to make dinner. Bacon and cheese quesadillas. Delicious. I scarf them down and make green tea for dessert. Sinking into my camp chair, I gaze out into the landscape before me. A sea of pines, lakes, streams, meadows, and the peaks and spires of Mount Jefferson. A truly spectacular camp.

For the first time in weeks, since we started this long road trip, I feel a tinge of longing for my friends and family back home. Faces, names, and familiar places I've come to know flash through my mind like old movies. My life is put into perspective, what a grand sufficiency it all is.

Even still, I'm not ready to go home. Not yet. As the memories pass, I remember there is much too much to see in this darned big ol' country of ours to go home now. When I reunite with Valerie and our truck camper, it will be time to head to Bend and the Three Sisters Wilderness. More hot springs, more trails, more backpacking. More exploring than I can possibly imagine.

I appreciate you, the reader. Thank you for coming along on this journey. It's entertaining to write, but it's even more enjoyable to know it will be read by people who care about wilderness. If I can inspire just one person to take that first step down a wilderness trail, or see for the first time the beauty in the bark of a tree, the frost on a windshield, or the dew on a blade of grass, then my life makes sense. How truly blessed I feel to live in this country, on this planet. How truly lucky we all are.

Day five.

I leave camp in a frenzy. A feeding frenzy. I seem to have camped in a mosquito metropolis. Stepping from my tent, clouds of the little vampires are immediately upon me. Packing quickly, efficiently, I move on. Five miles down trail, the mosquito clouds have disappeared. It's finally time to make coffee and breakfast. Surrounded by moss-covered pines, I retrieve Edward Abbey's *Desert Solitaire* from the top of my pack. I bring along this battered old paperback for two reasons. One: it's small and lightweight. Two: it's pretty much the best book ever written, at least on the subject of wilderness, philosophy, poetry and humor, not to mention spirituality. I've read it dozens of times. It never gets old, it only gets better.

I open the book to a random chapter. Cliffrose and Bayonets. As it turns out, Abbey is preparing coffee himself this fine morning, in his house trailer, working as park ranger and sole inhabitant of Arches National Park. On his morning stroll, he talks of cliffrose, cactus flowers, purple sage, and Spanish bayonets, all in his usual style of charm, wit, and grace.

Finishing the chapter, I take a sip of coffee and stare out over my surroundings. The Pacific Crest Trail lies fifty yards from the little coffee shop I've created in the woods. This is the season for through-hikers, and one just passed by. Sporting running shoes, headphones, and a tiny backpack, he wizzes past fields of wildflowers and huckleberries. Ultralight. Ultrafast.

I should shed some gear, I think to myself. Shed some pounds, log more miles. Then I consider he's probably not carrying a book, a leather-bound journal, camp chair, camp shoes, down jacket, fresh vegetables, frying pan, three person tent, full jar of peanut butter, and an SLR camera (with camera bag). Unnecessary items? Perhaps. Slowing me down? Definitely. But am I really out here to log miles, set a good pace, break records? Not really. Quite the opposite actually. Though I'd love to hike the entire PCT, 2,500 miles in all, I think I'd prefer to do it in chunks. Draw out the experience, span it out over a number of years.

You see, to successfully hike all 2,500 miles of the PCT, a rigorous schedule must be followed. In order to hike in the warmer months, when snow is not covering the trail, twenty- to twenty-five-mile days are essential. A tight schedule to be sure. Where would there be time for picking huckleberries and blackberries? When would I inspect the tiny flower gardens, follow coyote tracks, or explore that unmarked path that leads to who knows where? What about coffee breaks, afternoon naps, and general lollygagging? Hell, lollygagging is what I come out here to do! Kudos to the through-hikers, I think I'll stay here, enjoying my coffee.

Perhaps I'll stay the entire summer, right in this very spot. Yes. I'll pack in tables, chairs, bagel sandwiches, and a solar-powered espresso maker. Here I'll set up shop for the through-hikers. I'll offer hot espresso on the fly, with a walk-up window and brown bag lunches to go. Keep them hikers on schedule. Load 'em up with caffeine and carbs. I jot the elaborate business plan down in my journal for future reflection. Then I pack up and move on. I have my own schedule to keep, and this caffeine buzz won't last all day.

In a grassy meadow I set up camp for the night. Views to the west reveal ridges of mountains extending for at least fifty miles. I look at them longingly, I want to explore them all, but tomorrow will be my last day on trail. Then it's back to Breitenbush where I'll reunite with Valerie. There I'll soak, relax, and wash away the many layers of dirt and trail. Then it's back to truck camper life, the open road, and if I'm lucky, a cold beer in a cozy roadside cafe, salmon sandwich on the way. Fishwhich, they call them in Oregon. Fish, I could eat for every meal, and in Oregon fresh fish is abundant, caught from local rivers, sold in coolers on the side of the road.

Why do I think of these things when I'm days away from such luxuries? Why tease myself like this? It's interesting to watch these cravings come and go. We are constantly craving. That's what keeps the world in motion. Without cravings, we might all be sloths.

What's important is our awareness, our ability to watch these cravings. Only then we can decide which ones to give in to, and which ones to let pass by. Otherwise we become our cravings, we become slaves, eating our way to obesity, and buying every shiny new gadget we see.

Walking day after day, hour after hour, I begin to notice all sorts of cravings. There's no way of satisfying them, so I get really good at just watching them. Out here there's no minimart, no fridge full of food, no online shopping. So I keep on walking, watching, walking. Soon I start to realize that I am not these cravings. I am not these emotions, I am not these mood swings, I am not these fears, these hopes, these pleasures, these sufferings. I'm not even this person walking down the trail. I'm just along for the ride. So I sit back and enjoy the scenery. Enjoying the ride, the great movie. Life, unfolding right before my very eyes.

CHAPTER FOURTEEN

Three Sisters Wilderness, Oregon

BROKEN TOP MOUNTAIN TOWERS above our camp. Her peaks are adorned with rich color—royal red, specked granite, glimmering gold. Cloud formations appear out of nowhere, exploding in slow motion as they hit the jagged spires of Broken Top's peak. The display hypnotizes us for what seems like hours.

When the clouds dissipate, Mount Bachelor appears from the south, emerging like a ghostly apparition, a sharp contrast of white snow against black rock, hazy sky. Like most of Oregon's peaks, she's a volcano. Chunks of lava scatter her perimeter.

With year-round snow, Mount Bachelor is a

playground for gravity sport enthusiasts who come to ski her deep glaciers and steep couloirs. Bend itself is a playground, that is, for connoisseurs of human-powered sport. People who need nothing more than mountains, lakes, winding trails, and wild rivers for their recreation.

Bend boasts over 300 days of annual sunshine. There is enough mountain biking, hiking, backpacking, paddling, windsurfing, skiing, snowshoeing, and camping to last a lifetime. Free camping. As it should be. Gone are the dreaded NO CAMPING HERE signs. In their place something more sensible, a call for shared responsibility: NO CAMPFIRES, PACK IT IN PACK IT OUT, LEAVE NO TRACE. The problem is never camping, it's the trash irresponsible travelers leave behind, and the scars their campfires leave on the land. The answer, like always, is not stricter rules but better education.

Bend embraces quality of life. Simple things like good food, good beer, good people. In the breweries and cafes everyone is fit, attractive, full of laughter and smiles, eager to strike up conversation with a stranger. They love their city and it shows.

Staring out over the Three Sisters Wilderness, I sit with Valerie by my side, watching as a mountain stream delivers clean snowmelt to the base of our camp. Gone are the mosquito clouds of July—these are the golden days of August. Perfect time to be in the mountains. Long warm days, cool, star-filled nights, and that high summer feeling that the season will never end. Frolicking the rooftops of the world, lollygagging with the lilies, and loving as lovers do. Homeless. Jobless. Happy.

High in these alpine meadows we find it impossible not to fall head over heels in love. In love with each other. In love with life. Lovers are everywhere, kissing in the parks, swimming in the lakes, and rocking in their campers at night. Oregon. A sweet little word that rolls off the tongue, forever reminding us of the endless summer of 2014. The summer of love.

We pitch camp on the shore of a lake. The area is known as Green Lakes, but rather than green, our particular lake is turquoise, clear as the Caribbean, bright as the noonday sky. What causes such a color I have no idea, but it seems the colder the lake the bluer the water.

Valerie jumps in, then retreats quickly with a shriek that echoes off the basin walls. The lake is cold. Fed by glaciers. Frigid yet beautiful. She lies on the mossy shoreline to dry off, her wet skin radiating the glow of Indian summer.

The rest of the afternoon is wide open. No plans. Read, write, drink tea, swim, take a nap—all excellent options. As usual I'll choose not to decide. It's the lack of decision that relaxes the mind, offering the rare chance to call upon instinct rather than logic. Nothing against logic; it has its purpose, but instinct is what we're here to cultivate.

Take birds, for example. In the fraction of a second that occurs just before the entire flock changes direction in flight, no decision-making process can be observed. A unanimous decision appears to be made, instantaneously. There are no debates, no questions. Only a unanimous choice. The right one. A decision not premeditated, but made at the last possible moment. Nature's way.

What about fish? Do salmon deliberate whether or not to make the journey upstream to spawn, or do they simply go when it feels right? We know the answer. Studies like this are not new. Yet as humans, we continue to ponder every decision, every possible outcome. Must we plan out every detail of our lives, year by year, day by day, minute by minute? If every waking moment of our day is pre-planned, where's the room for instinct? We are losing one of our most fundamental skills.

What really separates us from our furry, feathered, and scaled relatives? Many things, to be sure. Let's take language—the ability to translate our thoughts into sounds and syllables. Advantage or a hindrance? With language, we've been able to construct entire networks of cities, and create gadgets that do previously unfathomable things. We can communicate and travel across the globe. We can write books, record history, create religions, start wars. But language as a hindrance? A disease? Impossible! Yet what if language was actually limiting our potential as a species?

Imagine if human beings lived by instinct rather than logic. How would this affect our world? Would we have made the same decisions leading up to now if we were not

capable of verbal communication? If we could not communicate verbally, how would we communicate? Is it possible that we once had the capacity to communicate on a
telepathic level, like the flock of birds, like the school of
fish? Could we still communicate at this level if it hadn't
been for language? I don't know. Again I'll choose not to
decide. Yet I can't help but think, what would the world
be like if we simply just *knew* all the right answers? What
if we never had to decide anything?

Let's take athletes. Sports like football, basketball,
soccer, mountain biking, skiing, whitewater kayaking,
kiteboarding, windsurfing, skydiving. When it's game
time and the ball is thrown, there is no time for a decision
-making process. Professionals who excel at their sport
realize this fully. To be the absolute best, words, thought,
and decision-making must take a backseat to instinct. To
second-guess is to fail. True pros make decisions instantaneously, in the moment, without any possible doubt.
When they are in the zone, they know exactly what to do,
and when to do it. Without thinking. Only knowing. Like
the flock of birds. Like the school of fish.

Is it possible that what we call talent is actually exceptional decision-making? Is it possible that exceptional
decision-making occurs with no thinking at all?

Thinking. This is what it always comes back to. Are
we over-thinking our way into madness and self-destruc-
tion? Have we lost our most basic skill, or just forgotten
it? Perhaps the mystics are right, if we could all quiet our

minds we might just become enlightened. We have much to learn. So much to learn from this Earth, before we figure out how to destroy it.

Happy hour.

Smoked oysters, crackers, hot sauce. Under Broken Top's shadow, it's the little things that satisfy the soul, the simple things. Take breathing, for example. Something we do all the time, and without thinking. Up here in the high country, breathing is invigorating. Even decadent! How often do we take the time to just sit and breathe?

Practices like yoga, meditation, and martial arts teach us to focus on the breath. People leave these classes feeling invigorated, but this should come as no surprise. Many of us wake up in the morning to a hysterical alarm clock, then jump in the shower, dress in a frenzy, drive through rush-hour traffic to get to work, work for eight hours, then leave work, drive again through more rush-hour traffic, pick up the kids, drop off the kids, run four yellow lights, making it just in time for yoga, so that we can finally BREATHE! Ahhhh, and now we breathe. Deep breaths. Big stretches. We try to focus on nothing, which of course is nearly impossible after the day we just had. But if we can forget about our busy life for just a few uninterrupted minutes, and focus on the breath, we can be transformed.

I treasure these long days of breathing and walking, indulging for hours in this kind of ecstatic breath. Taking in the sounds: flowing water, chirping birds, singing insects, rustling trees. The scents: fallen leaves, pine needles, dank soil. With every breath I become more a part of what surrounds me. We blend together until I can no longer feel a separation. At times it seems so ridiculously, so hysterically perfect that I can hardly contain myself. Then at the most crucial moment, something always happens: a raven flies close, our eyes meet, and for a fraction of a second we exchange some kind of information, something primal, beyond words. Then with the usual squawk of disapproval he flies off into the canyons below.

Who am I to try to understand the complex consciousness of the raven? I'm just a man. If this were my purpose I would have been born a raven. I breathe that in too, comfortable in my own skin, letting things simply be as they are.

The next morning we wake to misty skies. Slowly, a fiery ball of orange sunshine emerges over Broken Top Mountain, illuminating the low-lying clouds. Hours pass before we manage to pry ourselves from the bliss of the morning.

On trail again, our route drops us out of the high country and down into the wildflower meadows below. Losing elevation quickly, we follow a mountain stream as it flows down into a canyon, stumbling over waterfall after cascading waterfall, towards the valley floor. It's all gloriously beautiful, but our minds are already back in town. Rather than breathing in our surroundings, we're thinking of cold drafts and juicy burgers down at Deschutes, Ten Barrel, and the other dozen or so microbreweries back in Bend. We're thinking of showers, hot springs, and our soft mattress back at the camper. Luxuries that come with life in the front country. Luxuries we take for granted, yet find new appreciation for after days spent in the woods. These pleasures will be short-lived, we know this all too well. It's just a matter of time before the mountains call us to return, but for now nothing sounds better than Bend.

Back in town. We take six-dollar showers at the local recreation center, then head straight for McMenamins Old Saint Francis Schoolhouse for craft beer and Mexican food.

The joint is an old schoolhouse transformed into a brewery, restaurant, music venue, and the best part, Turkish soaking pools. This is a place I'd expect to see in a dark corner of Manhattan, down some secret alley among the ultra-hip. Or maybe in Vegas, obnoxiously overpriced in some ritzy casino, crowded with overweight tourists wearing Rolex watches. But McMenamins is in Bend, so the vibe is laid-back and easy-going.

We stroll over to the bar and each order a brew. Valerie goes with the Terminator Stout, I order a Hammerhead Classic Northwest Pale Ale. Classic or not, the pale ale is among the best I've ever tasted, taunting my nose with a spicy sweetness before settling into its Cascade hops, finishing with a zing holding not a trace of bitterness. Heaven in a glass.

We make our way over to a dimly lit table in the corner of the pub. Oil lamps adorn the walls and an old-school jukebox plays carefully selected cuts from the likes of Son Volt, The Beach Fossils, The Grateful Dead, and Bob Dylan. As the beer works its magic, carnitas nachos arrive, followed by seared ahi tacos. To die for. We order another round of beers and let the vibe linger a while longer as the high notes of Jerry's "Franklin's Tower" bounce around the room, painting smiles on the faces throughout. When we are finished enjoying, we ask the waiter for the bill. Thirty-three dollars. It's not enough. Insufficient compensation for this high a level of enjoyment. We leave a generous tip, gather up our towels, and head for the Turkish pools.

At the end of a dim winding hallway we find the ornately decorated room of blue artesian tiles where the soaking pools are hidden. Sounds of cascading water and distant music fill the room, and the ceiling is completely open to the night sky. I relax into the hot water at once, spying the Big Dipper overhead and several other constellations. The same ones I recognize from camping in the Three Sisters Wilderness just twelve hours before. I learn that this room is open to the sky year round and imagine soaking here in the winter, a light snow falling onto my face. I imagine soaking in a light rain, a thunderstorm, or during an eclipse. Taking another sip of my Hammerhead, I sink deeper into the warm water, soaking in the experience of McMenamins.

I have no idea how much time we spent at the hot pools. At some point we finally made it back to the camper, slid under the comforter, and opened up the skylight. Under the Big Dipper again, we drifted off to dreams of decadent abundance.

CHAPTER FIFTEEN

Ansel Adams Wilderness, California

A COLD WIND STINGS my face. It's late September and we are high in the Sierra Nevadas, just below tree line. Granite mounds surround us, shiny as silver in the blazing morning light. The sun warms my back as I face the wind, staring out into a life-sized Ansel Adams photograph.

The name of this place used to be the Minaret Wilderness, but it was changed back in 1984 to the Ansel Adams Wilderness, honoring both the man and the photographs he captured of the range—and rightfully so. Through his photographs he inspired millions to protect these lands. Now a person who has never stepped foot in this wilderness can look at an Ansel Adams photograph and feel something. Something primal. An urge deep inside their gut that calls to protect such sacredness at all costs. His photos convey the magic and beauty in a way that words simply cannot.

This is God's country, a 230,000-acre church created by no man. The energy here is thick, deafening, coming on as a rush, an undeniable shift in consciousness, a timeless essence as old as these rocks themselves. It feels like love itself.

A red-tailed hawk flies overhead, surfing the thermals of the morning wind. He is not hunting, not yet. Nor is he traveling. He is playing, arching his wings, creating graceful dives, then hovering in space, defying gravity. A surfer of the skies.

To my west I scan the area Valerie and I will be exploring: a wrinkled labyrinth of mounds, slabs, cracks and folds. Off we shall go...

Late afternoon, in a field golden with Indian summer, we make camp on the shores of Thousand Island Lake. Cliffs the color of polished nickel tower above our heads. Not since we left Colorado have we seen such a dazzling display of unbroken rock and sky. More beautiful now it seems than Oregon's Mount Jefferson, Mount Hood, or the Three Sisters. More beautiful even than the pristine beaches, misty rainforests, and towering redwoods of Northern California. But it seems that lately everywhere we go is more beautiful than the last. Perhaps we are simply falling deeper and deeper in love with the timeless beauty of the present moment.

Desert meets mountain. Rock meets sky. The landscape is so completely open that we can wander in any direction, hindered only by the crossing of a river or the occasional mountain range. Mostly we find smooth rock paving our way, extending for miles in all directions, a sea of granite rolling off towards the lost horizon. The sky is deep blue, sometimes even appearing black in the middle of the day, a stark contrast against the silver peaks and yellow sun.

This is wilderness to be sure. Black bear, coyote, elk, and bighorn sheep roam freely in this alpine expanse. Gone are the deep heady forests of the Northwest. We've found the crown jewel of North America. The Sierra Nevada. Unspoiled. Open. Free to all who wish to wander her sun-drenched valleys, winding rivers, and towering granite. Treading gently on her soil, I can now see why the likes of Ansel Adams, John Muir, and Theodore Roosevelt dedicated their lives to protect this earthly paradise. My gratitude is boundless.

Sandy beaches and golden grass sprinkle the edges of Thousand Island Lake, enticing us to wade out into her cool crystal waters. Valerie sunbathes on one of the beaches and I go for a swim. When I exit my skin dries instantly in the dry air, like in the deserts of Utah, and the swimming pools of Las Vegas.

At night the sky extends beyond our peripheral vision,

creating the most difficult of tasks: which part to focus on? Any moment of inattention and we may miss a shooting star, or some flash of light we cannot explain.

What are these mysterious flashes in the heavens? Planets? UFOs? God winking at us from above? We're not sure and find it better not to know, to live in the mystery. What do we really know anyway? We give names to things as if the names are a means to an end. But can we really know a star? Do the letters STAR describe the heavens any more than the letters WATER describe the ocean? Lose the words and the mystery returns. I find myself the most alive only when words and thoughts subside. That's where life begins. To truly understand a place like this, we must lay our thinking minds aside and simply breathe in the magic. Surrender to the mystery.

Day two.

We wake to a golden sunrise. Illuminated peaks cast their reflections on the lake. We make coffee, bacon, hash browns. It's windy but the rocks protect us, allowing us to lazily watch the day unfold. Back in town the rangers warned us about bears, insisting that we carry bear canisters to stow our food. So far the beasts have failed to appear. We've seen not a trace nor a footprint. After a few hours of lollygagging we pack up and hit the trail.

Like kids at Disneyland, we're dazzled again and

again on a magic carpet ride through a forest of sparkling peaks, golden domes, and towering ridges. Never
before have I seen such sculptured rock. The trail itself is
smoothly polished stone, yet trees cling to the rock, their
roots protruding deeply into the soil below. We stroll past
cliffs draped in exotic shades of copper, cayenne, chocolate. Every wall is worn smooth by glaciers that crawled
through here millions of years earlier. It's a wonder how
destructive forces can create such astounding beauty.

Over the next ridge we find Emerald Lake, sparkling
like a jewel set in stone, adorning the hand of Mother
Earth herself. Onward we go through a tunnel of rustling
aspens singing in the breeze, glowing in warm September
sunshine. We pass more lakes, each more beautiful than
the last, before descending into a rugged canyon where
the headwaters of the San Joaquin River flow. The mighty
river here is but a trickle, gurgling down a series of polished grooves in charcoal rock.

Downward. Eight hundred feet we descend. Then
climb. Then descend. That's how it goes in this type of
terrain. All day long we climb and descend, on a journey
both to the top, and down inside of the Earth. Here she
lies unabashedly naked for all to see. We are free to adore
her every curve with wild abandon, rendered speechless
by her ravishing beauty. We walk silently in a drunken
state of ecstasy down this trail of wonders. This city of
dreams.

We make camp in a protected meadow beside Summit

Lake, the water ablaze with evening light. Warming ourselves with hot apple cider, we absorb the last rays of the fading sun. We will sleep well tonight, as tired and happy backpackers do.

Day three.

No planes, no boats, no semis, no FedEx trucks, no garbage trucks, diesel trucks, air conditioners, construction vehicles, busy highways, generators, motorcycles, or helicopters this morning. Nothing but the wind. The howl of a coyote. Our breath. We breathe carefully so as to not disturb the rare, pristine alpine silence.

We live in a noisy world. It's no wonder we're cursed with the constant plague of incessant thought. Yet it seems that even the muddiest of waters clear when stilled. As our world becomes increasingly polluted with noise, silence is becoming our rarest commodity. It hits like a freight train when we find it, like a wall of silence.

We've become accustomed to the noise around us. We develop selective hearing, narrow our attention spans, or tune out altogether with headphones, iPhones, laptops, video games, and television. Why wouldn't we? How else to escape? What's the alternative? Ultimate insanity?

So we tune out. We turn on our device and turn off the world. In doing so we tune out the miracle we were born into, without even realizing it. Then one day we feel that something is missing. Something we cannot immediately identify. We have everything we *think* we need, yet still feel unfulfilled.

Then one day, if we are lucky, we experience a moment of clarity. Perhaps it's on a beach in Hawaii, or on the edge of the Grand Canyon, or high in the Rocky Mountains. "My God," we say. "How long have I been sleepwalking? Where have I been?" Then perhaps for only a second, we see that everything, absolutely everything is beautiful.

> *"Be still, and know that I am God."*
> *– Psalms 46:10*

In that moment we see through the eyes of God. We remember that everything *is* God. The mountains, the deserts, the oceans, the rolling plains, even our cities of asphalt and concrete, it's all God. It's all love. Everything is love. We've just forgotten.

Through all the noise and the madness, how could we have possibly heard what the Earth is so patiently trying to tell us? Now something as natural as silence has become increasingly rare. Wilderness is our only hope. The one place we can always come back to.

> *"Going to the mountains is going home."*
> *– John Muir*

For many, just knowing that wilderness exists is enough. That it is still possible to hop in the car and drive two hours, six hours, twelve hours—whatever it takes—to escape to a place that is still pure, free, and untouched by the hands of man. A land free for all who seek to fill that empty space inside, and bask in the presence of holiness. The Promised Land, Heaven, God, Source, Christ, Jesus, Buddha, Allah, whatever name you'd like to choose for *that which cannot be described*. The place we all come from and to which we will all return.

I must warn you though, do not bring your world into the wilderness. Leave it behind like an old pair of sneakers at the door. And if you can, go it alone. If you must bring a companion, I urge you to set an intention beforehand. It's all too easy to drown out the holy wilderness silence with chit-chat. Agree that you are going on a sacred journey, that you are going to church. If you must talk, try limiting conversation to things of the present, what's happening *now*.

Would you chit-chat about the latest gossip at work while sitting inside a church or monastery, or would you listen to the sermon? In wilderness, the sermon is delivered by no man, but rather by the rocks themselves, the air you breathe, the plants, the clouds, and the sky above. They regale a wisdom so ancient, so profound, that it permeates your soul deeply, using no words at all. Free at last from the incessant rumble of your busy world, the ancient wisdom of the Earth can finally be heard, sometimes resonating so deeply that tears fill your eyes, love fills your heart, and beauty blossoms from within.

So I walk, slowly, silently down the trail, hand in hand with my everlasting soul. A reunion with my childlike essence. Clean and pure. My thoughts drop like marbles, shattering as they hit the ground. In their place—truth, all-consuming peace, and a love that is not locked inside my own body, but everywhere, inside of everything and everyone. It was there all along. It can never die, only be obscured, lost, forgotten. Sometimes hiding out in the back corners of our being for years. Waiting to be let out.

Now that my marbles have been shattered, there is nothing left to do but to bask in this experience of pure love. Heaven on Earth. It's all happening right here. Right now!

The Earth, the mountains, the sky. I breathe them until I become them. All feelings of separateness dissolve and pure life force energy is all that remains.

I burst out laughing, realizing now that my body can crumble to dust but I will still remain as this love. I will still remain as this energy. This life-giving energy behind everything living and non-living. For when I die I'll become the dirt, nourishing the trees and plants, blooming into fields of wildflowers in the spring, flowing with the creeks and rivers down through the valleys, and filling up the lakes below. From the lakes I'll evaporate into clouds, raining down upon the plants below. I'll soak down into the Earth, filling the aquifers, filling the wells, and nourishing a thirsty child on a hot summer day. And I'll go on, and on, and on…

Day four.

Snow clings to the north-facing slopes. Last night's snowstorm was the first of the season. We're camped in a place called Dusy Basin just above 11,000 feet. The temperature is warm, the wind has died off, and we enjoy the morning's dusting under blue skies and dazzling sunlight. The hike to get here was through rough terrain, over grueling Bishop Pass. We've decided to spend the day here in this basin, among a scattering of small turquoise lakes. From our granite outcropping I count a dozen lakes and over forty peaks. Unbroken granite dominates the landscape and we have views in all directions.

There are no clouds. The wind, when it blows, brings with it suggestions of winter, the fragrance of snow. But it's not winter yet, this is Indian summer at its finest. Warm air. Clear, bug-free days. At night, temperatures fall down to around freezing, but our down bags keep us cozy. The sun warms our skin during the day, feeling never too hot or too cold. We wander this alpine playground in complete comfort, frequently resting on polished domes radiating the warmth of the blazing sun. Gone are the crowds of summer. In their place, the brilliance of fall silence.

In every direction I can see weeks of exploration. But right now, surveying from this bluff is enough, just knowing that it's all out there. I'm content with proof that it exists. That's the real purpose of these trips. Not to hike every trail, penetrate every canyon, or climb every peak, but to witness their existence. To verify that such beauty and magic still exist. I must see it for myself. Breathe in the mountain air, walk upon the delicate tundra, and feast my eyes on the very essence of beauty.

Like a love-struck teenager lusting over a high school beauty queen, I fall to my knees. My devotion dominates my very existence. To know her is to become her, submit to her, be devoured by her. My every pore infused with her beauty. I float back to camp, drunk like a bee returning from a field of spring wildflowers.

CHAPTER SIXTEEN

The Vegas Desert

A STRANGE LIGHT ASCENDS into the night sky. I watch it split into two. Then four. Then eight. Each travels in its own direction before dissipating into darkness. UFO? Some strange military operation? Possibly. The Nellis Air Force Bombing and Gunnery Range lies only forty miles from here. Strange things happen in the Nevada desert; I'll never know for sure.

A more familiar light, the moon, illuminates a forest of Joshua trees. There are hundreds of them. Their branches look like arms and legs suspended in motion. Some are running, others dancing. A jolly bunch. Moving in imperceptibly slow animation.

Down in the valley, fifty miles from here, I can see another light. The glow of a thousand hotels, strip clubs, twenty-four-hour casinos. Las Vegas. A fiery ball of energy pulsating through the desert night. A poignant cocktail of order and chaos, good and evil, God and man.

We need Las Vegas. Its strangeness lies somewhere on the outer fringes of our culture. A place for freaks: rattlesnakes and scorpions, ravens and vultures, kissing bugs and fire ants, you and me. All are welcome. All who are willing to live and let live, without judgment, embracing the colorful obscurity of coexistence.

"Just another freak in the freak kingdom."
– Hunter S. Thompson

CHAPTER SEVENTEEN

Highway 1

THE WAVES KEEP COMING IN.

One after another. Traveling thousands of miles to get here.

On a grassy bluff we gaze out over the blue horizon, pondering the vast wilderness of the Pacific Ocean. Sea, sand, and sun.

We arrived late this morning, after camping in a dark redwood forest a few miles north on Highway 1. Now we cannot convince ourselves to leave. From our perch we can see miles upon miles of rocky shoreline extending both north and south. Granite pinnacles penetrate the ocean's surface, adorning the coast with sculpture.

And the waves keep coming in.

Ribbons of perfect swells roll in one after another. On this rugged stretch of highway, no one is around. The only sound we can hear is the constant roar of the waves. The occasional cry of a seagull. And more waves.

A fine mist drifts in from the sea, coating our skin with moisture, watering the hillsides of grass, ferns, and manzanita.

And the waves keep coming in.

How long to stay at such a place when there is no schedule, no obligations, no timelines? An hour? A day? A week? Even thinking about it seems vulgar, absurd. We'll stay until we leave and that is that.

"A million-dollar view," I say to Valerie.

"Priceless," she says back to me.

Agreed. The finest resorts and hotels of California could not offer a view more perfect.

A vulture soars high above the shoreline, but from our bluff we are at eye level. With a swoosh, he buzzes our terrace above the sea. We exchange glances.

And the waves keep coming in.

A flock of pelicans, nine of them in all, fly in single file. They are headed north. To some secret fishing spot, I suspect.

And the waves keep coming in.

Our eyes are getting heavy. The sound of the ocean is all-consuming. The outgoing tide seems to be taking with it our thoughts and our cares, what little we have left.

Salty scents of the sea drift in on the ocean breeze.
And the waves keep coming in.
And the waves keep coming in.
And the waves keep coming in...

CHAPTER EIGHTEEN

The Ancient People

CANYON COUNTRY in the early spring. Cottonwoods just starting to bud. Strolling down a canyon fifty miles long, looking for water. Always looking for water.

Hidden in these walls are cliff dwellings, petroglyphs, pictographs, and kivas. The ruins you must seek out yourself, hiking miles, sometimes days to find them. There are no signs, no routes, no roped-off viewpoints. Not here. This is no Mesa Verde.

The ruins are far off-trail, hidden in alcoves, down unnamed side canyons. The early people thrived here for centuries. I can see why. They must have felt protected, building homes high up in the canyon walls. Away from enemies. They chose south facing walls, providing warmth from sun in winter, cool from shade in summer. Here they raised children, hunted food, and performed their daily duties. Passing the time, they made beautiful pottery and adorned their walls with artwork that still exists today. These petroglyphs (etchings) and pictographs (paintings) decorate the sandstone walls around their dwellings, throughout the canyons. Blending into the landscape, they are the only surviving mark of their existence.

Archaeologists say these cliff dwellers left rapidly. Perhaps their enemies, real or imagined, finally got the best of them, drove them out. Or maybe it was drought or famine. Whatever the reason, they moved on.

Now here I am—poking around their stone houses, many still intact after centuries, and sleeping in the canyons they once called home. Unlike them I have no enemies, I carry no weapons. Rather than sleeping high in the rock walls, I camp right on the canyon floor. In place of fear I only feel peace.

My reality is different. Safer. This is the easiest time to be alive. Poverty, violence, hatred, greed. Sure, they exist, as they have for centuries. These things are not new. The media is new.

Turn off the evening news. Better yet, turn off the TV entirely. Get rid of it. There has never been a safer time to be alive than right now. And since now is what we have, might as well enjoy it.

The cliff dwellers didn't need the media to tell them there were enemies lurking around every corner. This was their reality. Fighting was a way of life.

Climbing up a side canyon, I discover immediately a large area of ruins on a south-facing cliff. As the light fades, I climb as high as I can, reaching several of the lower structures. Potsherds and corn cobs scatter the floor. Petroglyphs and pictographs adorn the walls. Depictions of animals. Bighorn sheep. Deer. Others are more other-worldly, visions from dreams perhaps. Gods. Monsters. Demons. Below are three arrows, arranged vertically, all pointing down. Down towards what? I'm not sure.

Another wall exhibits a collage of handprints, small ones, like the hands of children. There are over a dozen structures. The highest ones I cannot reach. Too much exposure. A fall here would be fatal, and I'm far from medical help. These high sites are the best preserved.

I look back down-canyon and feel a rush of empathy for these people. The love in their hearts is the same as the love in mine. *We are the same.*

It's getting dark. I walk back down-canyon towards my camp. Frogs croak loudly in the stream. If you ever need water, wait until dark, listen for the frogs.

Day two.

More ruins, more petroglyphs, more artifacts. I'm

traveling through an ancient village. Around every corner more dwellings come into view, each more elaborate
than the last. It's the petroglyphs and pictographs that
I find most intriguing. A flying camel. A man with a frog
head. Spirals. Centipedes.

What are these strange animals? What are these
spirals? These figures? Visions? Figures to ward off evil
spirits? Appease the gods? Or just elaborate doodling?
We'll never know. The mystery is what makes them so
fascinating. I'm irresistibly drawn to them. Like guard-
ians of the canyons they have a life of their own.

Day three.

A cold silence blankets my camp. I make tea and look
at the map. I'm directly beneath a large ruin. The map
clearly states no camping right here. Whoops. I've not
seen a soul, but I break down my tent and sleeping bag
anyway, stowing them away in my pack. Now I'm not
camping.

The morning ensues. No one comes by. The wall behind me starts to glow in orange light. I should go inspect
the ruins, but I sit in silence instead. There will be plenty
of time for poking around. Right now the morning itself
is thrilling enough.

My mind turns back to the cliff dwellers. I picture
them waking each morning to the sun and the silence. I

imagine their breathing, slow and deep. I think of their eyes, peaceful yet alert. And their hearing, sharp like a cat. Under the constant threat of attack, an underlying peace must have prevailed. Predator and prey have always been the natural order of things. They built these cliff dwellings simply out of necessity, like birds building nests in the trees. There they felt safe.

What purpose does fear really have anyway? Does fear serve us?

We fear in times of peace. We fear in times of war. We fear in times of depression. We fear in times of prosperity. We fear losing our jobs, losing our money, losing our possessions, losing our loved ones, losing our friends. We fear our own annihilation. Is any of this based on reality? Or is it all in our imagination, based on some imagined future that isn't actually real at all? At least not yet.

Is fear simply a *dis-ease* of the mind? Do we need fear to survive, or just common sense? Does fear serve or sabotage? Did the cliff dwellers vacate due to real threats, or did their own fear eventually drive them to madness and mass exodus? Is it possible they left these pristine desert canyons for a fear that was only in their heads? So many questions, so little evidence. Much has been written, yet the truth remains a mystery.

The sun reaches me. It's time to go poke around some old ruins.

Camp.

Everywhere I look is golden rock and blue sky. I'm surrounded by twisted stone and vertical walls, like some kind of underground chamber, yet with an opening to the sky. A stream trickles close to camp, cool and clear. I gather water to make tea. In the shade of a juniper I sip, contemplating my surroundings, wasting away the day.

An hour passes.
The croak of a raven.
Another hour.

Clouds build on the horizon. A lizard with a long green tail sits beside me on a rock, eyeing me with caution. He takes a few steps in my direction, stares me right in the face. His sides are red, his underside green. Like a statue, I make not a move. Then he darts off in a frenzy across the hot desert sand.

This much silence is intoxicating. It comes on like a drug, intensifying awareness, amplifying sound. I hear a gunshot and my heart skips a beat, but it's just my cook pot ticking from the heat of the sun. I hear an entire family walking up the canyon, children playing and laughing, but it's just a flea buzzing in my ear.

It's the lack of sound that's so deafening here. The absence of sound. My other senses become heightened, a phenomenon that must be experienced to understand. With no sound at all, I focus on nothing. My mind becomes very, very still.

The air vibrates with a buzz that I can feel from the top of my head to the bottom of my toes. Love floods in. The light is intensified. Colors become more vivid. It becomes all-consuming. Difficult to contain. Can I love too much? What will happen then? I turn down the volume just a bit, more out of instinct than fear.

The breeze picks up, giving me a sudden chill. I move out into the sun and sit on a rock. The heat feels exhilarating.

Clouds build, thickening on the horizon.

"You've waited your whole life for this," I tell myself.

No words.

No words.

No words...

Day four.

I move slowly, careful not to disturb a single piece of pottery. This is a museum. I too am part of the exhibit, leaving my own footprints in the sand. Everything has its story—some are hundreds of years old, others just minutes. It's the greatest story ever told.

Alone. Longings and cravings stirring through my head—ice cream, soft skin, music, cold beer. They'll pass. The canyon darkens, but a full moon is on the rise. My focus shifts to a sliver of light, creeping down a canyon wall. Soon I will be bathed in moonlight. I'm lucky to be here. Lucky to be alive.

Strange thoughts pass like drifting clouds.

> Don't be one way,
> Wishing for another,
> Only to arrive at the new way,
> Wishing for the first.

Thoughts. Thoughts. More thoughts. Where do they come from? What do they mean?

Day five.

Sunlight creeps down the east canyon wall, bathing my tent in orange daylight. I've slept in, and instantly I'm famished. I move to the shade of a juniper and make tea and oatmeal. I'm several days in now. Decisions need to be made. Do I head back the way I came, or attempt a loop through an unnamed side canyon? A route requiring difficult navigation, possible scrambling, and a thirty-mile hitchhike back to my car. I won't make any decisions yet. Not until my pack is loaded and I take the first step. For now I have more important things to do. Like testing the walls for echoes.

I could stay out here for weeks. If it weren't for the allure of such things as cold beer in frosted pint glasses, burgers and fries, tacos. False promises, all of them, leaving me with a full belly but an empty soul. Eternally unsatisfied. Insatiably hungry. Always wanting more, more, more. The next fix. An endless, maddening process. But I allow these things to lead me back anyhow. I'm only human.

In three days I will leave this paradise of beauty and simplicity, for a world of desire and temptation. Yet each world makes the other all the sweeter.

> Without work could we enjoy the play?
> Without clouds could we enjoy the sun?
> Without sound could we enjoy the silence?

More thoughts. More words. Childish things.

Can I travel forever without longing for the comforts of home?

Always we want something else. We're sad and we wish we were happy. We're cold and we wish we were hot. We're in one place and we wish we were in another. Does our pain really come from our situation, or from our desire for something else? Change comes soon enough, does it not? Are we not just running in circles, chasing our own tails? Must we always be chasing the next better moment? As fast as we try to run, can we ever get to the future? And why the rush? Does the future really even exist? What if now is all we ever have? A movie with no beginning, no end.

My decision is clear. I will take the unknown canyon. A canyon which should lead, hopefully leads, out to the main road where I can hitch a ride back to my truck. If there is anyone there to give me a ride.

Onward. The side canyon is more beautiful, more spectacular than the last. More remote and more exquisite. But I've already seen more than I can possibly remember. For many weeks ahead, my dreams will be lush with visions of swirling sandstone and spirals, demons and gods, angels and monsters. It's all here in my memories. The memories that make up my life. The more I step out of my routine, the more I seem to create.

My life is a work in progress. But I have no regrets. If I regret anything, it's not doing more. Thankfully, I'm not done yet. I'm forty-one, almost forty-two. I've lived a life beyond any expectation I ever had as a child. But perhaps this is because I never had any expectations. Except to have fun. Fun is awesome, and my biggest motivator. Whenever I have a decision to make, I base my choice on what would yield the most fun. Because he who has the most fun wins.

Why should we ever stop having fun? I plan to have fun until it's no longer possible. Then I'll surely be ready to move on, recycle this old body back to the Earth. See what's next. How can it not be great? Perhaps even greater than this life. Until then I plan to have as much fun as humanly possible.

See ya on down the trail...

CHAPTER NINETEEN

Beneath the Surface

THE MOST SPECTACULAR DESERT country in all of the world lies between Moab and Hanksville, Utah.

Major cities are hours away. Tourists are busy exploring Arches, Lake Powell, Zion, and Bryce. Outside these parks is open land, free for wandering, exploration, bliss.

I'm camped at Angel Trailhead, just south of Hanksville, jump-off point for exploring the Dirty Devil River and all its canyons. Robbers Roost is my destination, lying somewhere out there, over the rim, a thousand feet below. It will be my home for the next four or five days.

Solo is a time to reboot. Step outside the real world. Stop talking, stop thinking, and start listening.

It's a time for gratitude and healing, both spiritual and physical. And it's a time to walk, simply walk, one foot in front of the other, and breathe in deep blissful silence. It will take a few days for my busy mind to slow its chatter, but it always does. So long as I'm patient, trust the process, and submit completely to a power much greater than myself.

Solo trips are where I remember who I am. Beneath this body, this face, this name. In the end, I know too well that these details will fall away, and all that will remain is this pure silence, this pure light. The same light I see in the eyes of a lizard, the eyes of a child, and the rocks, the plants, the lakes, the streams, the sun, the moon, the clouds, and the stars. As divided as we may seem, we're all in this together. In the end there is no separateness. No lines drawn between you, me, rock and tree. All of this I forget. Over and over I forget. Fortunately the desert is patient, reminding me again each time about the beauty, the silence, the light, and the miracle of all of existence.

Many of us have had similar revelations. Perhaps in a church or monastery, high on a mountaintop, or gazing into the eyes of a newborn baby. That experience when we stop thinking, even if just for a moment, and suddenly know—absolutely know—some overwhelming truth that we cannot put to words. But these moments are fleeting, for as soon as we try to put them to words, label them in some way, we lose grasp. We are back to thinking again and the moment is lost. The truth is enough.

Just knowing that it exists. So long as we don't try to turn it into something. Some thing, which it is not.

Tomorrow I'll go beneath the surface. Down into these sacred canyons. To seek out truth once again. . .

CHAPTER TWENTY

Robbers Roost Canyon, Utah

MY ROUTE BEGINS AS A TREASURE HUNT for rock cairns and markings. Clues that might suggest a route. Some way down, off this ledge, into the world below. The cairns disappear, but there are grooves and footholds chiseled into the rock. I should have brought a rope. Why do I always forget the rope? We slide down the sandstone, first my pack, then me. Grinding on sandpaper. We lose some fabric, a little skin, but make it. Getting back up will be another story. Another challenge for another day.

After an hour I'm on solid ground, taking off my shoes and socks at the banks of the Dirty Devil. The river is wide, nearly thirty feet across, but only ankle deep. The crossing is easy enough. I dry my cold feet on the other side and head downriver, towards the mouth of my canyon, Robbers Roost.

This is no trail. This is a bushwhack. I trudge through thick brush, deep sand, crumbling riverbank, mud. The walking is awkward and tiring, but the solitude is creeping in nicely. There is no sign of anyone. No one human. A childish possessiveness comes over me. *This place is all mine.*

The river comes to life. Ducks paddle the eddies. Herons fish the shoreline. An owl stares down, swiveling his catlike head in my direction, hunting. Wildlife flourishes. We are far from the progress of man. Like a revelation, an idea flashes through my head. *This place happens.* Everyday. Wild. Untamed. Free. A rare specimen of what Earth must have been like before man. An obnoxious species, are we not? With our cars, diesel trucks, motorcycles, ATVs, air conditioners, generators, airplanes, helicopters... It's not so much us creating the noise. It's our machines. They've become monsters.

A woodpecker taps away at a cottonwood just above my head. The only audible sound in the canyon. The tapping echoes like maracas off the stone walls. I come to an opening, a side canyon, and head in, thinking it could be Robbers Roost. More brush. More thorns. Thrashing through the tangle, the canyon closes in on me within a quarter mile. Dead end.

Retracing my steps back to the river we continue on.

The river and me. Moving together. Downstream. Silently and effortlessly.

Around the next bend a second opening emerges, much larger than the last. Wide and inviting, a stream of sparkling clear water flows from the mouth. Yes. This is my canyon. Jewel of the desert.

This place is a jungle. I expected dry sand and rock. Here everything is damp, lush, tangled. My feet sink into the marsh, slurping with every step. I struggle on like this for hours. Late in the afternoon, sore legs and a rumbling stomach, I find a spot to camp in an alcove, the only firm ground I've seen in miles. I wash the burrs and thorns from my beat-up legs in a nearby stream, then set up camp. As the light fades I begin to understand the depth of the solitude I've stumbled into. It's endless.

Barefoot, I take an evening stroll. The sand is still warm, massaging my tired feet as I walk. Mushrooms, reeds, and tiny flowers poke through the surface. Footprints are everywhere. Not just mine but an astonishing array of others. Some I can easily identify: large prints of deer, bobcat, coyote. Tiny feet and trailing tails of mice and lizards. Others are not so obvious. Strange patterns in the sand I do not understand.

What would our world be like without our machines? I try to envision our cities, bustling with people, but with no machines. As if someone flipped a switch, turning them all off at once, rendering them useless.

We love our machines, myself included. Without the automobile I could not have traveled here, at least not so easily. But at what point do our machines start to become a species of their own? When do they start taking over our lives? How long can we continue at this rate? What will our world be like two hundred years from now? Two thousand? At what point does the advancement of technology yield a diminishing return?

I am not alone with these questions. Others are questioning as well. *Less Is More* is a growing philosophy. Tiny homes and camper vans are now trendy. Passing fads? Or a real movement with the power to transform our way of thinking in a global way? These questions are always on the forefront of my thinking in places like this. Questions that beg to inquire: are we really so advanced or have we just made our lives more complex? Is simplicity a lifestyle choice or does our very survival as a species depend on it? Time will tell.

The sun goes down and I make a small fire, more for ceremony than for warmth. Gathering wood from around my site, I have it going in no time. The cottonwood and juniper burns sweet as incense. The glow is warm, enchanting. Dark now, the moon starts to rise. Light creeps slowly down the canyon walls. Tonight the moon will be full, but for now it remains hidden behind the rocks. Stars pop out one by one. First Venus, brightest star in the sky, then the seven sisters of Pleiades. As always, I can only make out six, the seventh sister elusive to the naked eye. Behind me, framed by towering canyon walls, appears the Big Dipper. The Great Bear. Always watching over me.

The heavens seem to be in order. I go for a stroll, still barefoot, through the soft sand. A shooting star flies overhead.

Every day this happens. Year after year. Decade after decade. Millennium after millennium. Time stops and I can feel my own mortality. There is deep love in these canyons. Radiating from everything, both living and non-living. How to even tell the difference? The moon is alive, very much alive. As are the stars, the rocks, and the flame of my campfire. All living, breathing parts of this world.

Wrapped in my goose down bag, I let my little fire fade out as I fall asleep. I dream of winding canyons, shooting stars, faraway galaxies.

Morning.

I wake to cold pre-dawn silence. Remembering the small pile of wood stacked next to my fire ring, I crawl out and spark a morning fire. It comes to life instantly, blazing with heat and light. I make tea, witnessing a new day rising. After a while the sun makes its grand entrance, touching the tops of the walls first, bathing them in bright orange light. It slowly fills the canyon, a process taking over an hour to complete. This is the most perfect of mornings. Sweetest time of the day.

When the light finally reaches me, the heat is stifling. I strip from down jacket to shorts and T-shirt and make breakfast. The day has awakened. It's anxious to get underway.

Afternoon.

The wind will not stop. I cannot tell where it is coming from. Which direction I walk doesn't seem to matter. I'm always heading into it. Sand is everywhere, in my eyes, my ears, my hair, my face. Stinging my skin, turning it to sandpaper. My mind and body are exhausted. Where to camp in a place like this? In my bewilderment I stumble into a cottonwood grove. It's not out of the wind, but at least out of the blowing sand. A big improvement.

Why do I do this? What am I doing out in this sandstorm?

> I march on.
> Sand pulls at my ankles.

> I march on.
> The scenery is grandeur.

> I march on.
> This sucks.

Evening.

Ah yes, evening. With each evening comes the bliss. The wind stops, creating a new world full of magic and enchantment. The canyon sighs with relief, filling the air with calm. Reprieve from the turmoil of the day. A reversal of sorts. In the mountains the nights are often cold and long, a time for cooking, cleaning, eating, and deep sleep. Not here. When the wind stops and the stars come out, that's when my day begins. It's like I've awakened from some sort of hazy dream. Late into the evening I stoke the fire, gaze at the stars, and wait for the moon. When it finally rises I'm bathed with midnight moonlight, bright as the midday sun.

I must remind myself that everything is working perfectly according to plan. But I also need to keep things in balance. Make sure there's not too much Yin and not enough Yang. Otherwise I'll need to make a change.

If this wind doesn't let up soon I'm getting the hell out of here.

CHAPTER TWENTY-ONE

Coyote Gulch, Utah

IT'S FOUR DAYS BEFORE MY BIRTHDAY. Valerie and I are camped right on the shore, by the sparkling water, in the dry desert air, under the brilliant blue sky.

Water trickles through the canyon. Birds, butterflies, frogs, and lizards mingle beneath the filtered shade of giant cottonwoods. The beach invites barefoot walking, sunbathing, lollygagging.

The sun has retired, but the rocks still hold the heat. The air smells sweet, and we sit with toes buried in the warm sand, enjoying tonight's feature presentation: an elaborate dance of flickering light projected against towering sandstone walls. Tomorrow we will explore waterfalls, arches, alcoves, hanging gardens, and the seeping springs of Coyote Gulch.

Deer stroll, frogs croak. Bats flutter out from their caves, diving at mosquitoes. Then comes the darkness. Strange echoes. Voices gurgling up from the stream. Rustling leaves, more frogs. Our hearts are light as feathers floating on a soft desert wind. We dream fairy tales into the night.

Morning.

Valerie's eyes sparkle clear and blue as she first exposes them to the light. The morning rings with mystery, magic, love, and abundance. Only when order and chaos reach perfect equilibrium can such brilliance occur. Eons of wind, water, erosion and time have created this masterpiece. It's a miracle.

We are here to witness at this most crucial moment in time, this rare event of Heaven on Earth. The search is over. We have arrived.

We are born searching. Constantly seeking something that we cannot name. Something we want so desperately but cannot describe. Here that searching is gone.

There's a primal wisdom deep within the fissures of the Earth. It's all right here. Ready for anyone who wishes to learn. A truth that has existed long before our species arrived, and one that will exist long after we are gone. There is much to learn. So very much to learn. I can feel it deep within the rock. Away from all the noise, the pollution, and the mindless chatter of incessant thought. The madness of our modern world. Her message is clear, and it's not one of gloom and doom, but rather one of hope: that the possibility still exists for global enlightenment. We are close. So incredibly close. And we have been for some time. All that's required is the simple flicking of a switch. Nothing will change but everything will be different. We shall continue on as before. Eating, sleeping, working, playing. But with new perspective. The perspective of God.

CHAPTER TWENTY-TWO

Last Post from the Road

DAYS COME AND GO like the pages of a book. It's late April, the day before my forty-second birthday. Ten months on the road. It all seems like a long, decadent dream. I've fallen gracefully into my natural rhythm. I wake when I awake, sleep when I'm tired, and the stars come out to greet me each evening like old friends. I'm in tune with them as they are with me. I don't know why this is so important, but it is. The phases of the moon. The orientation of the constellations. Venus. Ursa Major. The Pleiades. Orion. They allow me to feel a part of the universe, not separate.

In the mornings, I wake slowly as the sun begins its

journey across the open sky, back of beyond, over the canyons, hills, mountains, and plains. Soft music flows from our camper as I sip tea, effortlessly slipping from one dreamworld into another. Sometimes I cannot tell which is which, or if it even matters.

How will this all change when I transition back into the *real world*? I'm not even sure which one is real anymore. Will I bring this peace back with me? Can it survive in a busy world of schedules, deadlines, payments, and obligations? Will I remain part of the flow of the universe or will I fall back into the hustle and bustle of city life, feeling myself separate again? Time will tell.

Staying in the flow. I know this is the key. Remaining in touch with my body, the moon, the stars, sunrise, sunset, and remembering—knowing—that it's all me. And that the crystal clear waters of the desert canyons will still flow, even if I'm not here to witness them. That the moon, the stars, the constellations, and the planets will still make their journey across the night sky, even if there's a roof over my head. That I must only stop, look up, and look around to realize that everything, absolutely everything, is beautiful.

CHAPTER TWENTY-THREE

Big South Fork, Tennessee

"WHEREVER YOU GO, THERE YOU ARE."
There is wisdom in that old parable, and as far as I travel, as deep into the wilderness I push, there I always am—just the same. Searching. Always searching. For something out there, that I already know is inside of me. Something out there, to remind me that there is more to this life than what I can see on the surface. Something to remind me who I really am.

There comes a time when we must stop the search. Bring the journey to a halt, even if just for a moment, and reflect on how we got here. Observe the trajectory of where life has taken us, where it all started, and how far we've come. For me, that time has arrived.

I was born in the Midwest, in the rolling plains of Ohio. Farm fields, subdivisions, shopping malls—it was a far cry from the deserts and mountains I call home today. But there was wilderness. Albeit a different kind, it was wilderness just the same.

Wilderness: A region that is uninhabited,
or inhabited only by animals.

The little woods down the street from our family home was my first wilderness. Even before I was allowed to go down there on my own, I could feel the pull of this mysterious land beyond the pavement. A world full of endless possibility. Where the sidewalk ends.

There were creeks, frogs, salamanders, tadpoles, bluegills, snakes, spiders, turtles, and countless other critters. We'd spend hours down in those woods, just a few neighborhood kids, muddy and happy, catching fish, filling buckets with turtles, bugs, snakes, whatever we could find. It was freedom. It was paradise.

When summer came our days down in the woods lasted forever. Day after day we'd explore, pioneering new routes, erecting forts from discarded construction materials, digging trails with sticks, and staying out way too late. Dad's voice grew hoarse calling out to us from above, from the *other world*. Never once did we hear his calls.

We'd come plodding in just before dark, or just after, scrapes on our knees, holes in our jeans, late for dinner, late for ball practice, late for church, late for everything. We'd get into trouble, but we didn't care. The wilderness was worth it.

Even way back then I knew that nothing in this world was more important than the feeling I had down in those woods. But as the years progressed I grew bigger, and our little woods grew smaller. Our paradise was shrinking. Progress was moving into our neighborhood, and our woods was not part of the plan. Soon there was nothing left but a few trees and a polluted creek. Private property. No trespassing.

When time came for college I headed south, away from the suburbs and into the foothills of Appalachia. Eastern Kentucky University was the gateway to the Daniel Boone National Forest, Red River Gorge, and Big South Fork. A whole new playground emerged right outside my door. I bought a Texaco road map and started circling the names of all the places I wanted to explore: Indian Staircase, Twin Bridges, Slave Falls, Honey Creek. The place names dominated my mind. Pulling me from my studies. How could I rationalize studying indoors with all this wonder and mystery awaiting outside?

I majored in photography and went camping every weekend. With photography, I now had an academic reason to go into the woods. Weekend trips started to include Fridays, then Thursdays, sometimes Mondays. Classes were missed. The remaining days I'd spend in the dark-room, under the glow of a red light, watching my images slowly appear as apparitions, like fragments of a dream. I was hooked. Straight As lined my photography projects, my other classes suffered. I didn't care. The wilderness was worth it.

My sophomore year, Valerie graduated from high school and joined me at EKU. We spent our days as true romantics. Loading my tiny Mazda RX-7 with camping supplies, we'd race the backcountry roads towards my circles on the map. A new and exotic place each time. We'd camp beneath the stars, under natural bridges, on top of sandstone bluffs, in caves, and abandoned train tunnels.

Slowly we acquired gear, like backpacks and sleeping bags. As poor college students, all we had were school backpacks and heavy army surplus gear. As we light-ened our loads, we could travel deeper into the back-country and further from the roads. Fortunately we nev-er needed a tent. Never even considered one. The rock shelters and hollowed out cliffs that once housed Native American tribes provided all the protection we needed from Kentucky's frequent summer storms. In these an-cient dwellings we'd spend the night, thunder crashing all around us, making love to the flashing of the lighten-ing, as it illuminated the walls of the cave. We were safe, we were free, we were in love. In love with each other. In love with wilderness.

We flunked out together.

Then we moved back to Ohio to get married. Soon af-ter we moved to Colorado, never to look back. Until now...

I'm on a plane headed for Nashville, writing a story for *Backpacker* magazine. They need a story about the Big South Fork National River and Recreation Area, my old stomping grounds. Will the story get printed? Don't know. That's not why I'm here. The opportunity to revisit the wilderness of my youth was simply too good to pass up. It's been fifteen years. This will be my homecoming.

My flight is delayed. I retrieve my pack from baggage claim, stop at the store for camp fuel (not allowed on the plane), then drive two and a half hours towards the en-trance of Big South Fork.

The old road winds its way through tunnels of deep for-est, and crude tunnels blasted into the rock. Remembering the old RX-7, I reach for Valerie's hand, but it isn't there. A ping of loneliness. I should have brought her with me. Should have insisted that she come along. But then I re-member her words. "Go," she said. "Write your story."

I pull into the trailhead just before dark. Parking my rental car in an empty lot, I step outside. Immediately I feel as though I've entered a time capsule. The warm air, the moisture-rich soil, the smell of the oak trees, the moss-covered earth, the wet leaves and green foliage. It all brings me back. The magic, it's still here. Perhaps even stronger than ever.

I make my first steps down the trail and the ground makes no sound. Walking on a soft bed of wet leaves, I'm immediately enveloped by the sounds of the forest. The crickets serenade my return and at once I feel welcome. It's good to be back in these southern woods.

Through dark tunnels of rhododendron, I descend into mysterious alcoves, and rock houses the size of amphitheaters. In the fading light, everything drips with Tennessee dew. The trail is getting dark but I hike on, entranced by the night, my headlamp guiding me through the mist, deeper and deeper into the forest.

Hours later I find a place to camp—an enormous rock house with hanging gardens, dripping ferns, and a small stream trickling over a ledge, down into a pool. I make camp under the rock shelter, just as a crescent moon peeks through the trees and a few stars are revealed. The rain has stopped and the skies are starting to clear. There will be an eclipse tonight. I try to stay awake but drift off far too early.

Morning.

I wake and find myself underground. Like the wild canyons of Utah, these Tennessee caves and rock houses have been carved out of the Earth. Cliffs tower above and

I'm surrounded by a jungle of trees, roots, vines, and vibrant foliage. Everything glistens with morning dew. A dense fog rolls through, and it isn't until I step out from my rock shelter that I realize it's raining again. The air is hot and humid, and I enjoy the morning in only shorts and T-shirt, preparing morning tea in a brand new world.

It may be true that *wherever you go, there you are,* and as far as I travel I can never get away from myself. Yet it's also true that when I travel to places of unspoiled beauty such as this, I awaken something inside myself. The little soul from my childhood, the one that sometimes gets lost in the dark alcoves of my being, comes out to play.

I'm blessed and cursed with the soul of a child. One who is easily distracted, easily bored, and prone to depression if the boredom goes on too long. Yet when I nourish that inner child, my delight astonishes even myself. You see, there is this light. It's deep inside. We all know that it exists. It's everywhere, and in everyone, yet we do not always feel it. This light is the source of pure love. The light of being. The light of truth.

This light, I think it's worth searching for. Go find it. Perhaps you have already. Perhaps you are living it. If so, then I simply wish to remind you of its importance. Never take it for granted. Share it with others. If you haven't found it, then I urge you to go.

GO NOW.

What could be more important? What possible excuse could keep you from running wildly towards this blinding light? Living out the rest of your days in truth? If we are not living in truth, are we not living a lie?

Our inner child knows this all too well. Crawling deeper and deeper into the far corners of our beings, until we finally find truth. Or we stop looking altogether. Forsaking our inner child. Allowing the pure essence of our very soul to stay hidden for eternity, or at least until we die. And then we do die. Lonely and afraid. Repeating the process over and over until we finally get it. Until we finally remember, there is nothing more important than this light!

Night two.

Stir-fry. Ramen and peanut sauce. Dark chocolate and ginger tea. An owl hoots in the distance. Sounds of crickets. Running water. At a thousand feet above the sea, oxygen is rich and abundant, and the air is pleasingly warm. In Colorado I'd be wearing my down jacket by now, but here I sit comfortably in T-shirt and shorts. It's late September, the mosquitoes are gone, and I've got the place entirely to myself.

Tomorrow's hike should be easy. Six miles of trail. Then a night at Charit Creek Lodge, a backcountry abode accessible only by foot. Rustic cabins, lodge-style rooms, camping and hot showers. The main draw, besides the hot showers, is the southern home cooking, pie for dessert, and cold craft beer—as advertised on their website. Did I mention breakfast?

Rain. Rain. Blissful rain. With an air temperature of 70 degrees and 100 percent humidity, I find myself neither hot nor cold. Under a canopy of leaves, the rain comes down as more of a mist, my clothes damp but not dripping wet. My skin glistens, the bill of my hat drips, yet I feel no trace of a chill.

Spiderwebs sparkle like diamonds in the trees. Red, orange, and yellow mushrooms contrast strikingly against the dark soil. The wet leaves on the trail shine like oil on canvas beneath my feet. Like I'm walking through an unfinished painting.

I cross the steaming waters of Laurel Creek a dozen or so times. Crawfish, minnows, and frogs dart from my approach. In the middle of a crossing, suspended in time, I stop, realizing that as much as I change, this wilderness does not. She is no more and no less beautiful than my memory recalls from fifteen years ago. Undoubtedly, no more and no less beautiful than she was a hundred, a thousand, or even ten thousand years ago. Her delicate beauty remains, timeless.

I think of the Tennessee Citizens for Wilderness Planning, who helped to protect this land. If not for their years of fighting to get this wilderness protected, what may have been profit for a few is now a sanctuary for all.

The rain continues.

I hike on, passing more rock houses, more alcoves, more caves. Everything is covered in bright green moss, thick as shag carpet. At about three in the afternoon, I reach the lodge.

Founded in the early 1800s, Charit Creek Lodge is a wilderness gem, tucked deeply within the backcountry of Big South Fork. The creek was named in honor of a young girl named Charity, who drowned in its waters years ago. Kentucky is rich with southern lore like this.

The lodge exudes a charm of rare quality with its original structures. There are no roads, no cars, and no electricity. Oil lamps light the small cottages and dining areas. Propane runs the fridge and hot water heater, keeping the cold beer cold, and the hot showers hot.

The food is traditional southern fare: creamed peas, corn bread, cobbler, sweet tea, green bean casserole. On this foggy, rainy evening, I find the meal immensely satisfying.

After dinner the rain stops, and a soft evening glow illuminates the ranch. Perhaps tomorrow will bring the sunshine.

Rain. Rain. More rain.

The next day brings more unparalleled solitude. I pass waterfalls, rock shelters, natural bridges, and rushing creeks thriving with turtles, fish, crawfish, salamanders. At night, the soft sounds of light rain pat the rainfly of my tent. I drift off to sleep, still full of gratitude, for this experience, for this land that forever changed the course of my life. A land that showed me the magic of wilderness. It seems right to have come back to say Thank You.

CHAPTER TWENTY-FOUR

Wilderness,
The Gateway to the Soul

D OWN HERE, EVERYTHING IS BARE BONES. She lies on her back, naked for all to see, her rivets and ripples rising and falling at the pace of time itself. Her beauty is excruciating. Commanding. Raw. Unapologetic. Her perfection lies in her imperfection, in her flaws. This is where her true beauty is revealed.

What is beauty? Some say it lies within the observer. Where I witness a sparkling canyon of pristine beauty, others may see a desert wasteland, inhospitable, uninhabitable, intolerable, unprofitable.

Beauty is indeed a choice. Day by day, moment by moment, we choose love or hate, life or death, light or darkness. The seeds for both are contained within all things, both living and nonliving. It all depends on what we focus on. We create our own world. Focus on beauty and beauty you find. Focus on darkness and darkness will prevail. Beauty guides through the heart. Darkness through the mind.

How to see through the heart in a mind-dominated world? This is the challenge. We are at a crucial point of existence, and we have been for some time. Buddha knew it. Jesus knew it. Now it is you.

You are the messiah.

Do these words frighten you? Don't be ashamed, you are the chosen one. The one we've all been waiting for.

What will you do about it? Will you die for love? Will you fight for peace? Will you live for Truth? In every moment you have a choice. What will you choose? In the answer lies your destiny, and the destiny of all creation. This is how important you are.

"I choose light!" I can hear you say.

"I choose love!"

"It's the darkness in *others* that is the problem!"

"We must rid ourselves of the evil on this planet!"

Yes. Yes. It's all too easy to assume that the darkness in this world lies outside of ourselves. That others are to blame. Yet only when we learn to see the darkness inside of ourselves, can we hope to develop compassion for the darkness in others. For even the darkest of places contain the seed of light.

Such duality is embedded in the brilliance of nature. When we learn to seek light in the darkest of places, and brighten it with our own, only then can we hope to evolve.

Dark clouds have settled in, and the songbirds have stopped singing. A commanding presence takes over the land, calling me to listen deeply. Sitting perfectly still, I'm highly conscious of this brief moment in time. I'm free, at least momentarily, from the confines of modern society. Down here I'm homeless, penniless, jobless. I carry no ID, no credit card, no cash. I am nobody.

My situation is borrowed. A temporary reality. I know that I am confined to the modern world, and must adhere to its rules to reap the comforts that society provides. Yet I refuse to buy into them completely. I do not want to become dependent. Once that line is crossed, dependency becomes a crutch.

Wilderness is the place to understand this—to understand the universe. Life, death, love, hate, beauty, darkness—it's all here, tucked neatly between the sandstone's buttresses, fused into the grooves and cracks of the Earth. There's an order to all this chaos. I can see it so clearly now.

Our mind-dominated world is one of straight lines, boxes, and grids. Every last drop of our attention sucked out by an ever-expanding army of glowing rectangles. At times when I close my eyes, they are all I can see. I can feel it happening to myself, walking down the street, a zombie among the walking dead. Who are all of these people? What are they doing? Who am I? Have we all forgotten?

Then I know it's time to leave this world—just temporarily. Taking sanctuary to the mountains and deserts, back of beyond, where the pavement ends. To wilderness, the gateway to the soul.

Enjoy this Book?
Write a Review!

If you've enjoyed my book, the best compliment you can give is writing a review. As a self-published indie author, I don't have the advertising power of a major publishing firm. But you can make a big difference.

Honest reviews help other readers find me. It only takes five minutes and the review can be as short as you like.

If you'd like to leave a review on Amazon.com, search for my title, click on _Customer reviews_, then click _Write a customer review_. Simple as that.

Thank you very much.

Dirt-Worshipping
Tree-Huggers Unite!

_____

If you are interested in solo backpacking, or following along on my upcoming adventures via my blog, I'd love to connect with you!

Sign up for my mailing list and you'll gain access to:

- My ongoing travel essays.
- Exclusive photographs of wilderness areas from this book.
- Backpacking recipes, gear checklists, tips for finding your own gateway to the soul, and more.

You can sign up for my mailing list at
www.scottstillmanblog.com.

SAVE WILD UTAH!

SOUTHERN UTAH WILDERNESS ALLIANCE (SUWA)

SUWA is the only non-partisan, non-profit organization working full time to defend Utah's Redrock Wilderness from oil and gas development, unnecessary road construction, rampant off-road vehicle use, and other threats to Utah's wilderness-quality lands. Their power comes from people like you from across the nation who want to protect this irreplaceable heritage for all Americans.

If you'd like to get involved, please find them at **www.suwa.org**.

SOUTHERN UTAH WILDERNESS ALLIANCE

About the Author

Scott and his wife Valerie live in Boulder, Colorado. Whether backpacking, mountain biking, backcountry skiing, or kayaking, he travels with a pen and notebook and writes as often as possible.

You can find his blog and online home at **www.scottstillmanblog.com**.

If the mood strikes, send him an email at **scottmstillman@gmail.com**.

Bibliography

Coelho, Paulo. *The Pilgrimage.* Hammersmith, London: HarperCollins, 2005.

Fear and Loathing in Las Vegas, directed by Terry Gilliam. United States: Universal Pictures, 1998. DVD.

Ferris Bueller's Day Off, directed by John Hughes. United States: Paramount Pictures, 1989. DVD.

Indigo Girls. *Closer to Fine.* Epic Records, 1989. Compact disc.

Prine, John. *Long Monday.* Oh Boy Records, 2005. Compact disc.

Son Volt. *No Turning Back.* Rounder Records, 2009. Compact disc.

Watts, Mark. *Still the Mind.* Novato, CA: New World Library, 2000.

26994910R00129

Made in the USA
San Bernardino, CA
24 February 2019